The Young Naturalist's Handbook

First published 1978
Second impression 1978
The Hamlyn Publishing Group Limited
London · New York · Sydney · Toronto
Astronaut House, Feltham, Middlesex, England

ISBN 0 600 36579 4

Printed and bound in Spain by Graficromo, S. A. – Córdoba

The Young Naturalist's Handbook

Leonard Moore

Hamlyn
London · New York · Sydney · Toronto

Contents

Acknowledgements

Some of the illustrations in this book originally appeared in
the following Hamlyn titles: Bird Behaviour; Evolution of
Life; The Plant Kingdom; Snakes of the World; Geology;
Freshwater Fishing; Trees of the World; Fossils and Fossil
Collecting; Mammals of the World; Birds of Prey; Seabirds;
The Animal Kingdom; Animals in Danger; Natural History
Collecting; Seashells; A Guide to the Seashore; Ecology;
Garden Shrubs; Animal Migration; Birdwatching; Wild
Cats; Fishes of the World; Life in the Sea; Butterflies;
Garden Flowers; Plants for Small Gardens; My World of
Nature; Hamlyn Junior Nature Encyclopedia.

Special illustrations by Sarah Kensington; Kristin Rosen-
berg; Kay Marshall.

Introduction

As more and more young people go for their holidays to countries other than their own, they come to see plants and animals that are new to them. Someone from Belgium who explores the Scottish Highlands will be discovering as many new things as the English person who is taken to the Mediterranean shores for the first time.

This book aims to help keen naturalists to enjoy discovering the countryside of Europe and its wildlife. It is divided into sections, each one concerned with a particular habitat, as, for example, the seashore or the heath. To use the book, you should first turn to the section about the habitat that interests you, no matter which country you are in. There you will find information to help you understand more about it, how it is formed, perhaps, or how it can be studied. There then follows a fairly general picture of the kind of wildlife the habitat is likely to contain. The largest part of each section is about identifying the plants and animals you may see.

Of course, it is impossible in a small, pocket-sized book to include every living thing from every European country, but there is a useful selection of trees, shrubs, herbs, mammals, birds and sometimes fish, reptiles and invertebrates that may be found from Scandinavia to the Mediterranean. You will find the illustrations extremely useful and there are also short descriptions to add more hints for identifying. Don't expect to be able to put a name to everything you see—don't even try! The pleasure comes in using your eyes, watching and trying to find out the role that each living thing plays in its habitat.

Remember that a naturalist need never be bored, for wherever he is, he need only look around and there is something of interest to be found. And that is true, whatever your age.

Woodlands

Imagine Europe before there were any people. Much of the land would have been covered by forest, but very little of it remains today because for centuries men have been cutting down trees, especially in the less mountainous places. A great deal of the cutting has been to clear the ground for farming so that crops could be grown and cattle grazed.

Today, most of the large forests are either in the northern countries or up in the mountains where the land is unsuitable for farming. Luckily, however, there are still many smaller woods in the countryside of the lower lands of western Europe that we can enjoy.

Woods are either *coniferous, broad-leaved*, or *mixed*. In coniferous woods the trees bear cones and most of them are evergreen. Pine and spruce are trees of this type. Larch is a conifer too, but it is not an evergreen for it loses its leaves in the winter.

The broad-leaved woodlands consist of trees with much wider leaves than the needle-like ones of the conifers. Oak, beech and ash are examples of broad-leaved trees. They are also deciduous, which means that their leaves drop in autumn and new ones grow in spring, so broad-leaved woodlands are also called deciduous woods.

If there are both conifers and broad-leaved trees, the wood is said to be a mixed one.

In any wood one species of tree may be especially plentiful so we can talk for example of oak woods or pine woods, depending on which species is most common.

Most of the woods of England and the lower lands of western Europe are likely to be \of the broad-leaved kind, such as oak, beech or ash. There are some coniferous woods as well, not only natural ones but also those that have been specially planted, sometimes for their timber. However, most of the coniferous forests are in Norway and

Squirrels are common in coniferous woods.

Sweden, or in the mountains of Scotland, France, Germany, Austria, Switzerland and Italy.

Trees, like any other plants, will only grow where the conditions are suitable, and each species has its own particular needs. The kind of soil is important, for not only does a tree anchor itself in it, but the roots take up minerals and water from it. Heavy and damp clay soil is most likely to suit common oak trees, whereas the shallower soil often found over chalk is where beech woods are more likely to be found. Pines can grow on poorer and more acid soils, often in sandy areas.

Climate also affects the places where trees grow. Sweet chestnut trees, for example, need more warmth than spruce, so they will grow better in England and France, whereas the spruce will grow well in Scandinavia. Further south, nearer the Mediterranean, there are woods of other species of pine and it is even possible to find some woods of olive trees.

Deciduous woods are lovely in spring.

Life in Woodlands

In a wood it may be difficult for certain plants to get all the light they need, and this affects the time of year when they flower and come into leaf.

In the first few months of the year, from January to April and the beginning of May, broad-leaved woods such as oak woods are light places since the leaves of the trees have not yet grown and shaded the ground beneath them. During these early months, many smaller plants grow fast. They flower, fruit and build up their food stores while they are able to make the best use of the light that is available.

In an oak wood, for example, primroses and golden-yellow celandines bloom early; violets and bluebells a little later. By mid-May, the trees are in full leaf so that although any light that does filter through is very bright, there is bound to be more shade than when the trees have no leaves.

From then on, fewer plants can be found in flower. The dull, yellowish green flowers of wood sage and the small pink or white flowers of the tall, slender enchanter's nightshade are two that can often be seen and ivy may be found in flower as late as November. A visit to a wood once or twice each month, even through the winter, to record those plants that are in flower makes an interesting project and never fails to produce one or two little surprises.

Another fact to notice in woods is that the plants seem to form layers. The most obvious one is the *tree layer* containing the largest plants in the wood. There may also be a *shrub layer* in which woody plants can be found that are not as tall as the fully-grown trees. There might be hazel, possibly holly and maybe saplings of the larger species of trees, or any type of plant that will not die down completely during the winter.

Plants that do die down make up the third, or *herb layer* (also known as the *field layer*). Herbs are plentiful in an oak wood. Many species can be found making the most of what light there is, growing where moisture and temperature are more steady and where they do not have to stand up to the buffeting by wind and rain that the trees have to face.

Finally, close to the ground, are the mosses and lichens of the *ground layer*.

This *stratification*, or growing in layers, can be clearly seen in oak woods but not always so easily in other types. In beech woods, for example, the trees come into leaf much earlier than oak so for a longer period the wood is very shady. The shrub and field layers are much poorer and may even be absent. This is so in pine woods, too, where the shade is dense for most of the year.

Stratification can be found in birds as well as plants. Some, such as wood pigeons, nest high in the trees. Other birds, woodpeckers for example, nest and feed in the lower parts of the trees. The various species of tits are more often seen in the shrub layer, but even there each species may prefer its own particular part.

Plenty of birds spend much of their time on the ground and blackbirds and wrens are likely to be heard scuffling among the dead leaves there.

(You might try searching for insects and see whether there is stratification in them too.)

The search for food takes up a large part of an animal's day, since it is only plants that are able to make their own food from water and carbon dioxide by harnessing the sun's energy. Some animals therefore obtain the food they need for energy by eating the plants. But these plant-eaters, or *herbivores*, may then, in turn, be eaten by other animals, the *carnivores*, so that the energy passes to them. Sometimes these carnivores may themselves be eaten by larger carnivores, and so on.

An avenue in a beech wood.

These steps make up a *food chain* and every food chain begins with a plant. As an example, we may think of a leaf being eaten by a little caterpillar. Along comes a small bird which eats the caterpillar. Maybe it is on the ground and fails to notice a fox out hunting and so we have the food chain of leaf– caterpillar – small bird – fox. But small birds eat other things besides caterpillars, and foxes kill creatures other than small birds to eat. So many different food chains may join at different points to make *food webs*.

Trying to work out food webs needs patience and keen observation. Often there may be clues which will help if the animals do not show themselves. Footprints can help, once you have learnt to recognise them. Owls make pellets of the food remains they cannot digest

and bring them up from their stomach to drop on the ground. Taking these apart is fascinating; it shows which animals the owl has recently caught.

A whole wood will show many food webs, with plants and animals depending upon one another. Each type of wood will have different plants growing in it and the animal life will not be the same in each.

Try studying a single tree, for what goes on in the whole wood also goes on in one tree on a much smaller scale. That single tree may show a number of food chains. It

A typical food chain.

will bear leaves which provide food for various insects, the bark may well be covered with other simple plants such as algae, lichens and possibly mosses, and large fungi may grow on it.

Insects live on the tree, often in large numbers, not only eating the leaves, but the fruit and seeds as well. Certain wasps and beetles lay their eggs so that the larvae hatching from them may burrow into the trunk to feed on the wood. Birds such as woodpeckers will search out and feed on many of the larvae.

Even mammals, like the squirrel, may find the tree a useful home, while beneath the soil among the roots worms and beetle larvae may find their food supplies.

An old oak tree is a very convenient home for the following species:

1 oak bark beetle: 5mm; makes long tunnels under bark of trees.
2 nut weevil: 6–7mm; lays eggs in nuts.
3 goat moth: 95mm; feeds on wood of tree; strong, goat-like smell.
4 great spotted woodpecker (*see page 17*).
5 oak gall wasp: up to 4mm; adult has long wings; gall up to 20mm.
6 earthworm: common segmented worm; basic food for many other animals.
7 stag beetle (*see page 20*).

Things to look for in Woodlands

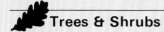 **Trees & Shrubs**

Common oak
Quercus robur
Durmast oak
Quercus petraea
Both species are large trees, up to 30 metres high, found throughout most of Europe. Common oak more often on clay soil, durmast oak are more likely on acid soils. Leaves of both have lobed edges. Acorns of common oak are stalked, but those of durmast oak are not and are attached directly to the twigs.

Beech
Fagus sylvatica
Up to 30 metres high. Smooth grey bark. Buds long and slender and bud scales hang for some time after leaf has unfolded. Leaves vivid pale green when young, becoming deep green later. Nuts enclosed in prickly husk which splits into four lobes when ripe. Large proportion of nuts are useless and will not grow. Found wild over most of Europe. Beech woods very shady with little undergrowth.

Silver birch
Betula pendula
Up to 25 metres high. Bark smooth and white, but with rough, black patches when older. Branches droop gracefully. Twigs brown. Leaves small, roughly triangular, with toothed edges. Catkins can be seen for most of year but do not grow long until spring and summer. Seeds in ripe female catkins are small and winged. Found in Europe, especially on light, dry soils and heaths.

Olive
Olea europea
Young trees slender, but old ones often very twisted and strangely shaped. Leaves evergreen and leathery. Flowers small, white, sweet-smelling. Fruit green at first, turning red and bluish-black, but not ripe until winter. Oil is taken from soft outer part after hard stone is removed. Found in Mediterranean countries.

Larch
Larix decidua
Up to 50 metres high. A deciduous conifer. New leaves bright green, darkening later. Leaves in tufts of thirty to forty, really short shoots. Female flowers pretty clusters of pink scales, sometimes called 'larch roses', ripening to egg-shaped cones same year. Native of mountains of central Europe but grown in Britain since seventeenth century.

Sycamore
Acer pseudoplatanus
Large tree up to 30 metres high. Bark smooth and grey at first. Older bark rough and fawn-brown. Buds green in winter. Leaves have five lobes and reddish stalk. Flowers in long hanging clusters. Fruit has two seeds, each with a wing spreading sideways. Native of central and southern Europe, but grows easily in northern Europe also.

Norway spruce
Picea abies
The Christmas tree. Up to 40 metres high. Bark greyish-brown with a reddish tint. Evergreen. Leaves narrow, 10–20mm long, soft mid-green colour, pointed but not sharply, and on tiny short shoots. Cones hang downwards; long, brown, 100–150mm. Native of north and central Europe and on mountains farther south. Introduced to forests of Britain.

Ash
Fraxinus excelsior
15–25 metres high. Smooth grey bark on young branches; older branches rougher. Buds black and bursting late (end of April). Leaves long, with central stalk and leaflets each side of it. Fruit with single seed and wing, flat and dry. Bunches of these may hang on tree until well into winter. Grows in most European countries.

Hornbeam
Carpinus betulus
Up to 30 metres high, but usually less. Bark smooth grey, marked with a network of lines. Sometimes mistaken for beech, but buds are shorter and edges of leaves are doubly toothed. Fruit in clusters, each having two seeds carried on a three-pointed wing 25–40mm long. The wood is the hardest grown in Europe. Found from southern Sweden to the Pyrenees.

Rowan
Sorbus aucuparia
Slender tree up to 15 metres high. In woods and on mountains higher up than any other tree. Bark grey and smooth, but marked by bands of pores. Leaves with six to seven pairs of leaflets on central stalk, each having toothed edge. Masses of white blossom in May. Fruit are berries, green at first but becoming bright orange by August. Also called mountain ash. Found in most of Europe, especially in northern areas.

Elder
Sambucus nigra
Shrub or small tree up to 10 metres high. Bark brownish-grey. Twigs stout with many small, raised pores; brittle and containing much soft pith. Leaves with central stalk with five or seven leaflets attached. Flowers creamy-white in large clusters opening in June. Fruit small purplish-black berries. Native to Europe from Scandinavia southwards.

Spindle
Euonymus europaeus
Shrub or small tree, 2–6 metres. Mostly grows on chalk and lime-rich soil. Twigs green and with buds in opposite pairs. Flowers small and greenish-white. Fruit four-lobed, green at first but becoming pink. Splits to show seeds with bright orange coat. White wood was once used to make spindles for spinning wool into thread. Found in Europe from Sweden to Spain, Sicily and Greece.

Hazel
Corylus avellana
Usually as a shrub, 1–6 metres high, with several stems. Bark smooth, brown, peeling easily into strips. Leaves very broad and slightly hairy. Male catkins like lambs' tails, shedding pollen in February. Female flowers like small, scaly buds with tuft of three red threads at top. Fruit a nut with woody shell held in a green, leafy cup. Found in central and southern Europe.

 # Herbs

Violet
Viola riviniana
Small plant, with stems that may look as if they are creeping. Leaves heart-shaped with toothed edges. Flowers violet, but sometimes white, with a curved *spur* behind. Some species of violet are very sweet-scented, but those of woodlands often have no scent. Common in Europe from Scandinavia to Portugal.

Wood Anemone
Anemone nemorosa
Erect plant, 60–300mm high. Stem smooth or slightly hairy. Three leaves on stem, each having a short stalk and very deeply lobed so that each leaf is almost split into three parts. After

flowering, leaves with longer stalks grow from underground stem. Flowers single, white but sometimes pinkish, 20–40mm across; five to nine sepals which look like petals. Common, often in large numbers. Found in north of central Europe.

Primrose
Primula vulgaris
Small plant, often growing at the edge of wood, or in clearings. Leaves long, up to 150mm, oval, narrowing to stalk. Flowers pale yellow, 20–30 mm across, each on a hairy stalk up to 100mm high. Petals notched. Usually several flowers on each plant. Found in western Europe, from Norway to Portugal.

Bluebell
Endymion non-scriptus
Grows from a bulb. Smooth, narrow, strap-shaped leaves, 200–450mm long, erect at first but lying flat after flowering. Flowers small, bell-shaped, blue, occasionally white. Many of them on one side of smooth stalk 200–500mm high, drooping at the tip. Found in Netherlands, Belgium, France and Britain, and possibly introduced into Spain and Italy.

Ground ivy
Glechoma hederacea
Low plant with creeping and rooting stems. Leaves heart-shaped, 10–30 mm across with blunt-toothed edges. Flowers bluish-violet; narrow trumpet-shaped with two lower lips at mouth; small clusters where leaves join stalk. Grows mainly on damp, clay soil. Found in most of Europe.

Cuckoo-pint
Arum maculatum
Short plant, 300–500mm in height. Leaves shaped like large, dark green glossy arrowheads up to 200mm long, sometimes spotted with black. Flowers very tiny; separate male and female ones clustered on stalk with soft, purple spike at the end; all surrounded by a pale green hood, edged and sometimes spotted with purple, called a *spathe*. Fruit bright scarlet and fleshy clustered at end of stalk. Found in most of Europe to southern Sweden.

Ivy
Hedera helix
Climber, up to 30 metres, but often creeps along ground and covers large areas. Very small roots on stems to help cling on. Stems sometimes very thick. Two types of leaves; on flowering stems they are oval, pointed, with smooth edges. Non-flowering stems have leaves more or less triangular with three or five lobes. Flowers green, on stalked clusters at end of stem. Found in most of Europe.

Red campion
Silene dioica
Fairly tall plant with some shoots growing along the ground, but those with flowers grow upright to 300–900mm high, covered with soft hairs. Leaves oval with pointed end, in pairs. Flowers pink, five petals, each with a deep cut in the end. No scent. Seed pod like a vase with tiny teeth rolled back so that seeds can be scattered when plant is moved by wind. Common all over Europe.

Herb Robert
Geranium robertianum
Leafy plant, 100–500mm high, with thin stems, usually branched; green but often tinged with red. Leaves made up of five leaflets with deeply cut edges. Flowers bright pink, 90–120mm across. Pollen orange. Whole plant has a strong smell. Found in most of Europe except northern Scandinavia.

Greater stitchwort
Stellaria holostea
Low plant with weak, branching stems, often trailing along ground.

Leaves very narrow, 40—80mm long, in pairs opposite each other. Flowers white, five petals, each one split to halfway down its length. Very common all over Europe. Also called satin flowers or adders' meat.

Betony
Betonica officinalis
150—600mm tall. Upright stem with leaves in pairs on opposite sides. Leaves 30—70mm long, fairly narrow with blunt-toothed edges. Flowers reddish-purple, small, trumpet-shaped with ends of petals showing at mouth, in tightly-packed bunches near top of stem. Found on heaths and grasslands as well as woods throughout most of Europe.

Foxglove
Digitalis purpurea
Tall plant, 0·5—1·5 metres high. Leaves large, oval, covered with soft hairs. Flowers trumpet-shaped, twenty to eighty on a tough hairy stem, reddish-purple but paler inside with deeper purple spots. A drug is obtained from foxglove for treating some heart diseases. Found in western Europe, from Norway to Spain, but not in Italy or Switzerland.

Yellow bird's nest
Neottia nidus-avis
Low plant about 300mm high. No green colour at all. Stem and scaly leaves yellow or cream with waxy appearance. Top of stem droops when in flower. Feeds on decaying plant remains. Grows mainly in beech and pine woods. Found in Europe southwards from Scandinavia.

Honeysuckle
Lonicera periclymenum
Climber, up to 6 metres, but may be low and trailing. Twines clockwise. Leaves oval, pointed but not sharply; smooth edges, in pairs. Stem slightly hairy or smooth. Flowers in clusters at end of stem; creamy-white with purplish tinge; long tube with lip at mouth; very sweet smelling. Fruit are red berries. Found in most of Europe.

Bracken
Pteridium aquilinum
Very common tall fern spreading by underground stems. New shoots grow up with leaves curled inwards; bright green covered with fine brown hairs. Leaves long, up to 1·5 metres or more, edges very much divided, growing almost horizontally from stem. Found throughout Europe and in mountains up to the tree line.

 # Fungi

Stinkhorn
Phallus impudicus
The young fungus is shaped like an egg, covered with thin skin, with fawny-brown jelly inside. This soon bursts open and a white, spongy stalk grows up to 100—200mm high with dark brown or blackish slimy mass of spores on top. *Very* unpleasant smell which attracts flies. These carry off the spores, leaving a lace-like top.

Species of *Russula*
Medium to large fungi. Typical toadstool shape with flattish cap which is often brightly coloured; some species bright red, but others may be purplish, yellow, orange, or dirty green. Gills white, with a waxy appearance. Flesh brittle and easily broken. Found in late summer and autumn, some species in pine woods and others in deciduous or mixed woods.

Honey fungus
Armillaria mellea
Usually grows in tufts of as many as twenty toadstools on stumps and dead trees, but also at the foot of many kinds of living trees. Cap 60—150mm across; may be bowl-shaped;

15

dull yellow at first becoming darker brown and covered with dark brown scales. Stem has a ring of skin, white with yellow edge.

Birch bracket
Piptoperus betulinus
Grows only on birch trees. Shows first as a white lump on trunk which later enlarges to a thick, semicircular bracket jutting out. Silvery grey on top, white beneath. No gills. Spores drop from tiny tubes. There are many of these and the ends may be seen as holes on the underside. Fungus may become very hard when old.

Death cap
Amanita phalloides
Grows in broad-leaved woods, especially beech. Cap 70—120mm across, pale yellow with a greenish tinge. Gills white. Stem white, swollen at the base and covered with loose skin. Ring of white skin around stem. Deadly poisonous.

Edible boletus
Boletus edulis
Called *cèpe* in France, *Steinpilz* in Germany. Large, heavy-looking toadstool with cap looking like a large bun, brown on top and white or pale green underneath, 60—120mm across. Stem thick, pale brown. No gills; many pores instead. Found in broad-leaved woods, especially beech. There are many kinds of boletus; some are very good to eat but others have an unpleasant taste.

Fly agaric
Amanita muscaria
Medium-sized toadstool with flattish cap when fully grown. Cap red with white patches of skin dotted over it. Ring of skin around stem; base swollen with several rings of skin around it. Poisonous. Fungus was once used for killing flies by breaking pieces up in milk; this attracted flies and poisoned them.

Birds

Willow warbler
Phylloscopus trochilus
Length 110mm. Exactly like chiff-chaff in appearance, but song is different. Willow warbler has a very musical song, starting on a high note and gradually getting lower by a gentle series of notes. Common in woods with undergrowth. Both chiff-chaff and willow warbler are in Europe only during spring and summer. During winter months they migrate to Africa.

Chiff-chaff
Phylloscopus collybita
Length 110mm. Small bird, common in woods with undergrowth and more often heard than seen. Sings perched in trees and song is easy to recognise since it sings its name 'chiff-chaff' in a monotonous way. Bird has greenish-brown upper parts, light below. Blackish legs. White stripe above eye. Similar in appearance to several other warblers and best identified by song.

Nightingale
Luscinia megarhynchos
Length 160mm. Shy, dull-coloured bird, brown above and creamy-brown underneath. Best known for the beautiful song of the male during spring evenings. Also sings during the day to warn other males from its territory. Keeps well hidden in bushes, and nest is built in thick undergrowth. A spring and summer visitor to Britain; migrates to Africa for winter. Not seen in Scandinavia.

Treecreeper
Certhia familiaris
Length 120mm. Brown speckled appearance on upper parts, white below. White stripe over eye. Thin, pointed, slightly downward curving beak. Very active little bird found in

most kinds of woodland. Often seen clinging to tree trunk and climbing jerkily upwards in a spiral around it, probing in bark for insects. When finished at one tree drops down and starts at bottom of another.

Tawny owl
Strix aluco
Length 380mm. Well camouflaged with brown and fawn plumage, although in some countries it may be much greyer. Large dark eyes set in front of head as in all owls. Hunts at night, catching small mammals and birds. May make hooting noise 'hoo-oo-oo' or sharper 'kee-wick' but never both together. Found in woods and parks and is the most common owl in Europe.

Long-eared owl
Asio otus
Length 350mm. Well camouflaged with brown and fawn plumage. Yellow eyes. Recognised by long tufts of feathers on head which are held upright when disturbed like ears, but these are not the true ears which cannot be seen. Sits very upright on branch. Common in coniferous woods, where it hunts at night and roosts in the trees during the day.

Short-eared owl
Asio flammeus
Length 375mm. Similar colour to long-eared owl, but 'ears' are much shorter and not easy to see. Hunts during the day, mainly in more open country, feeding chiefly on field voles. Migrates southwards to Africa and Mediterranean countries in winter, but some stay in southern England and Ireland.

Great spotted woodpecker
Dendrocopos major
Lesser spotted woodpecker
Dendrocopos minor
Length 200mm. Bold pattern of black and white. Two white patches on back. Red patch on head and under tail. Seen in broad-leaved and coniferous woods. Lesser spotted woodpecker similar but smaller. Wings and back with white bars, not patches. Found in broad-leaved woods only. Both species drum by rapidly tapping dead branch with beak.

Green woodpecker
Picus viridis
Length 300mm. Green back and red patch on top of head. Grey-green underneath, Young are spotted. Sharply-pointed beak. Seen mostly in broad-leaved woods where there are clearings. Does not often drum. Call is rather like a laugh. Often seen on ground eating ants. Hops clumsily.

Nuthatch
Sitta europea
Length 140mm. Often seen climbing down tree trunks headfirst. In broad-leaved woods and also in parks. Upper parts of body bluish-grey, white throat, reddish-brown underneath. Black eye-stripe. Short tail; rather large head and long, pointed beak. Can open nuts by jamming them in bark of tree and hammering at them with its beak until they split.

Woodcock
Scolopax rusticola
Length 350mm. Found in woods with clearings and wet ground. Very difficult to see on ground because of protective colouring. Reddish-brown with darker bars on head and underparts. Long beak. Eyes set high on head and well back so it can see all round. Most likely to be seen flying at dawn and dusk. If young are in danger, female may carry them to safety in her feet or between her thighs.

Coal tit
Parus ater
Length 100mm. Common, but shyer than blue tit (*see page 223*). Some-

times seen in flocks with other tits feeding together, mainly in winter. Recognised by glossy black head, white cheek patches and white patch on back of neck. Rather dull greyish-brown back and lighter underparts.

Crossbill
Loxia curvirostra
Length 140mm. Male red, tinged with orange. Young males duller. Female yellowish-green. Both have dark brown wings and tail. Usually seen in small flocks and always in coniferous forests where the birds feed on the seeds of pine, larch, spruce, etc. which they take from the cones with their unusual shaped beak. The tips of the beak are crossed, the hooked tip of the top one crossing over the bottom.

Goldcrest
Regulus regulus
Length 90mm. The smallest European bird. Common in coniferous and mixed woods, but also in hedges and on heaths and commons, outside the breeding season. Greenish colour with bright orange or yellow-orange crest on darker head. Young birds do not have coloured crest. Nest made like a basket of feathers, moss and spiders' webs hanging from branch of conifer.

Crested tit
Parus cristatus
Length 100mm. Greyish-brown back, light underparts, but easily identified by black and white crest on head. White cheek patches, black curved line behind eye. Crested tits are found mainly in coniferous woods where they eat insects which live on the pine trees and sometimes the pine seeds. May be seen with coal tits and goldcrests in winter.

Jay
Garrulus glandarius
Length 350mm. Much of body

pinkish-brown but top of head is black and white, and rump is white. Bright blue patch on wing, barred with black. Quite noisy with harsh voice. Common in broad-leaved woods. Collects acorns in autumn and buries them for winter food. Forgotten ones grow, so jays help the spread of oak trees.

Mammals

Common shrew
Sorex araneus
Length of body about 70mm, tail 50mm. Small mammal with long, pointed snout. Dark brown fur on back, greyish-white underneath and light brown along sides. Active both day and night. Has a shrill, squeaking voice, or sometimes a gentle chatter. Found in meadows as well as woods throughout most of Europe but not Ireland or most of Spain.

Edible dormouse
Glis glis
Medium-sized rodent with body up to 190mm long and tail up to 150mm. Fur grey above and white below. Tail bushy. Looks rather like a squirrel. Good climber and feeds on seeds, shoots and fruit. Sometimes enters gardens and houses. Active at night. Hibernates during winter. Found mainly in central and eastern Europe.

Bank vole
Clethrionomys glareolus
Small, mouse-like mammal but with more rounded head and blunter snout than mouse, also smaller ears and shorter tail. Light, reddish-brown on upper parts, cream-coloured underneath. Body length 80–120mm, tail 40–70mm. Makes shallow burrows and ball-shaped nest of grass. Feeds on seeds, fruit and leaves. Absent from Spain and most of Italy.

Grey squirrel
Neosciurus carolinensis
Similar shape to the red squirrel but a little larger. No ear tufts; more rounded head. Fur grey, but may be more reddish in summer. Found mainly in deciduous woods. Introduced from America. Common in Britain where it has taken the place of the red squirrel in the deciduous woods; almost absent from the rest of Europe.

Red squirrel
Sciurus vulgaris
Body length up to 280mm, tail length up to 240mm. Medium-sized rodent, reddish-brown (some much darker); white underparts. Bushy tail and ear tufts. Good climber and can travel fast in trees. Climbs down trunks of trees head first. Nests, called *dreys*, ball-shaped, made of branches and lined with grass. Prefers coniferous woods. Rarer in Britain than grey squirrel.

Pine marten
Martes martes
Slim body 420–520mm long, tail 220–265mm. Most of body brown but can best be recognised by yellow fur on throat and chest. Hunts at night. Able to leap about easily among the branches. Becoming rarer. Found in coniferous and mixed woods over much of Europe, except southern Spain.

Red fox
Vulpes vulpes
Body length up to 770mm, tail 300–500mm. Looks like a reddish-brown dog with white underparts. Very pointed muzzle and bushy tail, often with white tip. Hunts mainly at night, but may sometimes be seen during daylight. Found in Britain and most of Europe in woods, meadows and even in suburbs. Feeds on small mammals, birds, carrion and plants. Den is a burrow.

Badger
Meles meles
Heavy body about 700mm long and short tail. Grey colour over much of body, black underneath. Short black legs and feet. Bold pattern of black and white stripes on face. Long snout. Badgers are very shy animals, coming out of their underground dens, or *sets*, only at night. Each set is a system of tunnels with many entrances.

Roe deer
Capreolus capreolus
Small deer, only about 700mm at the shoulder. Coat red-brown in summer and greyer in winter; white patch around tail shows up well in winter. Male has small, branched antlers. Often seen in ones or twos rather than in large herds. Barks when surprised. Common over most of Europe, but very shy.

Fallow deer
Dama dama
Similar shape to red deer, but smaller; up to about 1 metre at the shoulder. Reddish-brown coat in summer with white spots. Coat is greyer and spots are less clear in winter. Male has branched antlers, wide and spade-like at the top. Fallow deer prefer open woodland and parks where they can graze as well as eat the leaves of shrubs.

Red deer
Cervus elaphus
Large mammal standing 1·5 metres at the shoulder, males larger than females. Reddish-brown coat in summer but a grey-brown in winter. Mainly a woodland animal, but in Scotland found on open moorland in the mountains. Males have branched antlers during breeding season which they later lose and grow afresh each year. Young have spotted coats. Red deer live in herds.

19

Wood lemming
Myopus schisticolor
Body length 85–95mm. Tail 15–19 mm. Small rodent, smaller than the better-known Norway lemming. Grey over most of body, but reddish-brown patch on back. Very short tail. Usually lives in coniferous forests where it may tunnel in moss layer close to ground. Active mainly at night. Found in Scandinavia.

Wild boar
Sus scrofa
Large, dark coloured, bristly pig with large tusks which point upwards, especially in males. Young are paler brown with light stripes along length of body. Males usually alone, but several females and young may be seen together. Can often be heard snorting. Not likely to be confused with any other animal. Found over much of Europe, but not in Britain.

Wild cat
Felis sylvestris
Similar to domestic cat, but rather larger and heavier. Greyish colour with dark stripes and dark rings around tail. Most active in the early morning and late evening hunting mice, small birds, insects. Lives mainly in the mountainous parts of Europe, including northern Scotland. Although similar in appearance, it is not the ancestor of the domestic cat.

Beaver
Castor fiber
Largest European rodent with body nearly a metre long, plus broad, flat, scaly tail. Short legs and webbed feet. Short ears. Found in open woodlands alongside rivers and lakes, mainly in Scandinavia but a few also in southern France and Germany. Very shy and seen mostly in the evening. Walks clumsily but swims well. Dams streams with branches, stones, etc. Feeds on water plants and bark of trees.

 **Invertebrates**

Stag beetle
Lucanus cervus
Length up to 75mm (male). Largest of the British beetles. Found throughout Europe, usually in deciduous woods, for adults feed on sap of oak trees. Male has large jaws which look like stag's antlers. Female has much smaller jaws. Eggs laid in rotten stumps of oak trees. Larvae feed on the wood for three to five years before pupating in soil.

Wasp beetle
Clytus arietus
Length 9–13mm. Called wasp beetle because colour and behaviour mimic wasp. Body black with yellow bands across wing cases. Orange-brown legs. Long antennae. When on tree trunk, beetle scurries over it in a slightly jerky way and taps its antennae, both kinds of movement being very much like those of a wasp.

Forest shield bug
Pentatoma rufipes
Length 11–13mm. Found in deciduous woods and orchards throughout most of Europe. Body shaped like a shield, broad and flattened. Greenish-brown with bright orange spot near centre of back. As with many bugs, part of the fore-wings are hardened as wing cases, but transparent ends show at rear, crossed over each other.

Green lacewing
Chrysopa septempunctata
Length up to 40mm. Delicate insect with slender, pale green body and transparent wings covered with a network of veins, making them look like lace. Eyes golden. Not very good flier and often found at rest on leaves in woods and hedges. Feeds on green-fly and other small insects. Adults of some species of lacewing hibernate in houses in winter.

Scorpion fly
Panorpa communis
Length 15mm. Small insect found around edges of deciduous woods, especially damp ones, or hedgerows. Male looks very fierce with its head drawn out to a long beak and its tail turned up over its back like the sting of a scorpion. Quite harmless. Wings transparent with a number of dark blotches.

White admiral
Limenitis camilla
Medium-sized butterfly with wingspan up to 60mm. Found in deciduous woods throughout Scandinavia and central Europe and parts of Britain. Upper surface of wings brown with white band on each wing from front to rear. Underside orange and grey-brown with white bands and dark spots near outer edges. Caterpillars of white admiral feed on honeysuckle and hibernate during cold months.

Purple emperor
Apatura iris
Medium-sized butterfly with wingspan up to 60mm. Wings mainly brown, but male has a purple sheen on the upper surface. Lives in deciduous woods throughout most of Europe. Eggs are laid on willows and larvae feed on the leaves. Adults fly around the tallest trees in the wood and this is where mating takes place. May also be seen near ground feeding on nectar.

Pine hawk
Hyloicus pinastri
One of the many species of hawk moth. Found in pine forests of northern and central Europe, but not often seen in Britain. Large moth with wingspan of 85mm. Usually flies at night, feeding on honeysuckle and other long-tubed flowers. Rests during day on pine trunks where its grey and brown colouring make it well camouflaged.

Red underwing
Catocala nupta
There are several species of red underwing moths, but they are all very similar. They are fairly large moths, up to 75mm wingspan. The forewings are mottled grey and grey-brown and provide good camouflage when closed. The hind wings are dark brown and crimson and can be displayed quickly to frighten off enemies such as small birds.

Key
Throughout the identification sections, the following abbreviations have been used:

BL=body length, excluding tail
Ht=height

L=overall length
m=metres
mm=millimetres
(m)=male
(f)=female
Ws=wingspan

Trees & Shrubs

Common oak
Ht up to 30m
(p12)

Durmast oak
Ht up to 30m
(p12)

Beech
Ht up to 30m
(p12)

Silver birch
Ht up to 25m
(p12)

Sycamore
Ht up to 30m
(p12)

Olive
Ht 10 – 15m
(p12)

Norway spruce
Ht up to 40m
(p12)

Larch
Ht up to 50m
(p12)

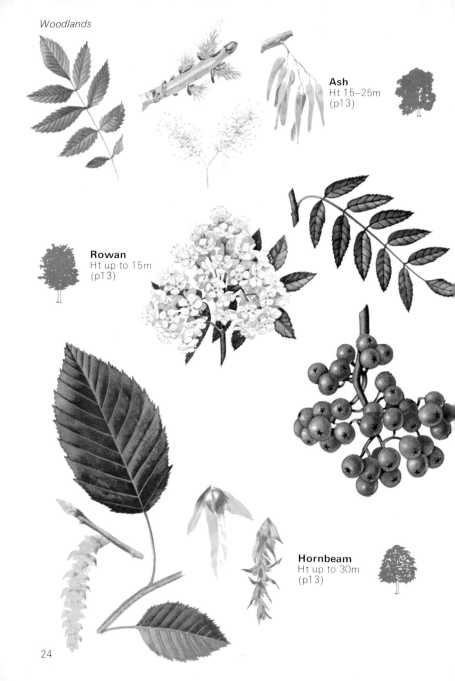

Ash
Ht 15–25m
(p13)

Rowan
Ht up to 15m
(p13)

Hornbeam
Ht up to 30m
(p13)

Elder
Ht up to 10m
(p13)

Hazel
Ht 1 – 6m
(p13)

Spindle
Ht 2 – 6m
(p13)

Herbs

Primrose
Ht up to 100mm
(p14)

Violet
Ht 20 – 200mm
(p13)

Bluebell
Ht 200 – 500mm
(p14)

Wood anemone
Ht 60 – 300mm
(p13)

Ground ivy
Ht 100 – 300mm
(p14)

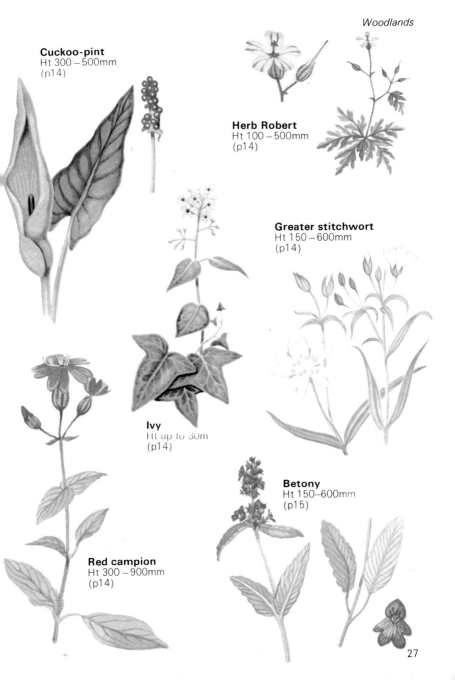

Cuckoo-pint
Ht 300 – 500mm
(p14)

Herb Robert
Ht 100 – 500mm
(p14)

Greater stitchwort
Ht 150 – 600mm
(p14)

Ivy
Ht up to 30m
(p14)

Red campion
Ht 300 – 900mm
(p14)

Betony
Ht 150–600mm
(p15)

27

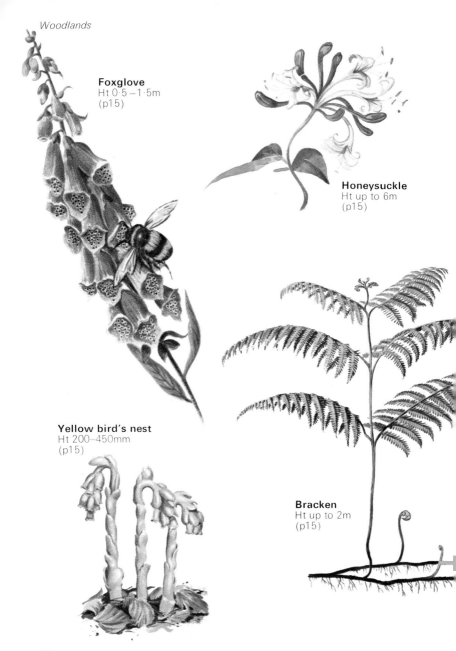

Foxglove
Ht 0.5 – 1.5m
(p15)

Honeysuckle
Ht up to 6m
(p15)

Yellow bird's nest
Ht 200–450mm
(p15)

Bracken
Ht up to 2m
(p15)

Fungi

Russula emetica
Caps up to 100mm across
(p15)

Stinkhorn
Ht 100 – 200mm
(p15)

Honey fungus
Cap 60 – 150mm across
(p15)

Birch bracket
50 – 300mm across
(p16)

Edible boletus
Cap 60–120mm
across
(p16)

Death cap
Cap 70–120mm
across
(p16)

Fly agaric
Cap 60–160mm
across
(p16)

Birds

Willow warbler
L 110mm
(p16)

Nightingale
L 160mm
(p16)

Chiff-chaff
L 110mm
(p16)

Treecreeper
L 120mm
(p16)

Lesser spotted woodpecker
L 150mm
(p17)

Tawny owl
L 380mm
(p17)

Long-eared owl
L 350mm
(p17)

Short-eared owl
L 375mm
(p17)

Coal tit
L 100mm
(p17)

**Green
woodpecker**
L 300mm
(p17)

**Greater spotted
woodpecker**
L 230mm
(p17)

Nuthatch
L 140mm
(p17)

Woodcock
L 350mm
(p17)

Crossbill
L 140mm
(p18)

Crested tit
L 100mm
(p18)

Jay
L 350mm
(p18)

Goldcrest
L 90mm
(p18)

34

Mammals

Common shrew
BL 50 – 80mm
(p18)

Edible dormouse
BL 130 – 190mm
(p18)

Bank vole
BL 80 – 120mm
(p18)

Grey squirrel
BL 245–300mm
(p19)

Pine marten
BL 420–520mm
(p19)

Red squirrel
BL 195–280mm
(p19)

Red fox
BL 580 – 770mm
(p19)

Badger
.BL 610 – 700mm
(p19)

Roe deer
BL 1–1·25m
(p19)

Fallow deer
BL 1·75–2·5m
(p19)

Red deer
BL 1·75 – 2·5m
(p19)

Wood lemming
BL 85 – 95mm
(p20)

Wild boar
BL 1 – 1·5m
(p20)

Wild cat
BL 475 – 800mm
(p20)

Beaver
BL up to 1m
(p20)

 Invertebrates

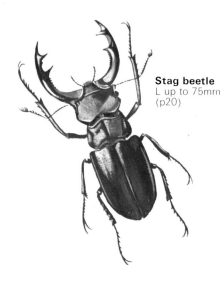

Stag beetle
L up to 75mm
(p20)

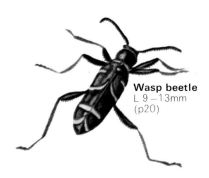

Wasp beetle
L 9–13mm
(p20)

Green lacewing
L up to 40mm
(p20)

Forest shield bug
L 11 – 13mm
(p20)

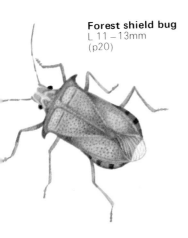

Purple emperor
Ws up to 60mm
(p21)

Scorpion fly
L. 15mm
(p21)

Pine hawk
Ws 85mm
(p21)

White admiral
Ws up to 60mm
(p21)

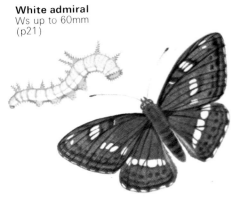

Red underwing
Ws up to 75mm
(p21)

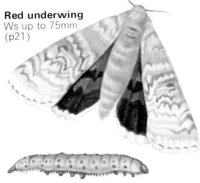

43

Lowland Meadows & Hedges

Much of Europe's grassland has been made by clearing trees from woods and forests and allowing cattle and sheep to graze on the land instead. If the cattle and sheep were removed and the grazing stopped, new trees would begin to spring up again and scrub would develop. In time, the land would become forest once more, so to a large extent it has been Man who has produced the grassland.

So important is grass, because it is the cheapest food for plant-eating animals, that farmers may often plough a field and sow grass seed to make pasture for their cattle. These pastures usually last for only a few years and are known as *leys*, while others are more long-lasting.

44

Cattle grazing in meadows.

and some grow well in places where others would die. A few kinds can grow close to the sea, whereas others grow better high up in the mountains. (Information about the alpine meadows will be found in the section about mountains.) Meadows do not consist only of grass, of course. There are usually very few trees in them, but there is often a wealth of other small flowering plants.

Very often, the boundary around a meadow is made by a hedge. The word 'hedge' means different things to different people, depending on where they live. To some it is made of stone slabs, to others it may be an earth bank. Some hedges, called 'dead hedges' are made by knocking stakes into the ground and weaving thin branches around them. But hedges to most people are the boundaries that are made of living shrubs and trees.

These are the hedges of most interest to naturalists because they are so much like small woods in many ways. In fact, many hedges really are the remains of a piece of woodland that was left when the rest of it was removed.

There may well be a small bank at the base of the hedge and sometimes a narrow drainage ditch as well. Conditions will be different on each side of the hedge because usually one side is likely to be sunnier and warmer than the other. One side may possibly be damper than the other, and these varied

When grass has grown tall, it can be cut and dried for hay, which can be used as winter feed for the animals. In the past, a farmer would use the word 'meadows' for the fields of grass that were to be cut for hay, and 'pastures' for those where his cows could graze. Nowadays, a field may be used for both hay and grazing and so the two words do not have such clear-cut meanings.

Grass needs plenty of moisture to grow well so areas with the heaviest rainfall will be likely to grow better grass than drier parts.

Some fields lie alongside rivers and in the past were flooded every so often. These *water-meadows* produced very good grass for cattle, but they had to be well-drained because good food grass cannot grow well in soil that is water-logged.

There are many species of grass

Hedges may be hiding a variety of wildlife.

For wild animals, hedges have many uses; they provide food, cover, nesting sites and look-outs. But the hedge and the meadow cannot be separated. The life of one extends into the other.

conditions will result in different plants flourishing on either side of the hedge.

Life in Meadows & Hedges

Meadows have few trees or shrubs in them, whereas the hedges that surround the meadows are made of them. There are many animals that live in the hedges and venture out into the meadows for their food. This is especially true of many birds, which need trees and shrubs in which to nest and as high points from which to sing.

The insects, seeds and small creatures of the meadow may well be the main source of food for the inhabitants of the hedge, so it is useful sometimes to consider the meadow and hedge together when studying the animal life of the lowland grassy areas.

Beneath the grass of the meadow lies the world of the soil. The soil grains have been made from broken-down rock fragments, but there are also plant remains in it, and a thin film of water around each particle. Among all these particles live vast numbers of living plants and animals, many so small that they can be seen only by using a microscope.

There are bacteria and many other kinds of single-celled plants and animals. These will be food for slightly larger animals which may still be too small to be seen easily with the naked eye.

However, there are plenty of larger animals in this dark world and all of them have some effect on the flowering plants anchored in the soil by their roots. There are earthworms in unbelievable numbers, eating their way through the soil, helping the air to move around under the surface and turning it over like Nature's ploughmen.

It has been estimated that in the soil of old grassland there may be up to 7·5 million worms per hectare, and they all make casts on the surface. These casts are made of the

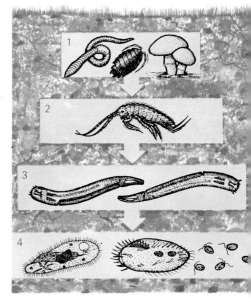

The world of the soil

1 worms, woodlice, toadstools, etc
2 springtails
3 nematodes
4 single-celled animals

soil that has passed right through the worms' bodies. Charles Darwin, the greatest of all naturalists, once collected worm casts on measured areas of land and calculated that over a year they came to about 25 tonnes on every hectare!

There are other underground animals, however, that do considerable harm to the meadow. The larvae of click-beetles are called wireworms because their bodies are worm-shaped and their skin is very tough. They feed on the roots of plants and, unfortunately, are very common beneath the surface of meadows. The real trouble comes when old grassland is ploughed up and then the new crops that are planted are often killed by the wireworms.

Other troublesome larvae are leatherjackets, which later in their lives change into crane-flies, often better known as daddy-long-legs. Many birds dig the leatherjackets out in spring and eat them. They may also eat the white, fat larvae of cockchafers which are common in grasslands.

A mammal which is adapted for living beneath the soil is the mole. Its presence in a field will be shown by piles of loose soil on the surface. These mole-hills are made from the soil which the moles push out as they tunnel.

The chief food of moles is earthworms and enormous numbers of them are eaten every day. When worms are plentiful, the moles may store them in special underground store rooms. The worms are bitten in such a way that they cannot move, but still remain alive, and so when the mole needs them they are fresh to eat. Moles may spend quite a bit of time above ground, but they are rarely seen, because as they hear footsteps, they are able to burrow down very quickly indeed.

Meadows normally contain several species of grass, but throughout the autumn, winter and spring only their leafy shoots can be seen. Although it is possible to identify them at this stage, it is much easier in the summer when the flowers develop on them. They are not colourful flowers since their pollen is carried by the wind so they do not need to attract insects. Common species in meadows include rye, cocksfoot and fox-tail grasses, but there are many others. Some grow well on chalky land, others where it is damp. Often the grass grows thicker where it is grazed.

Animals graze in different ways. Sheep crop grass closer to the ground than cows and therefore a farmer will vary the length of time different animals are allowed in the field.

There are always other flowering plants in a meadow besides grasses. Yarrow and white clover are two which cattle like, and these types of plant seeds will be deliberately added to the grass seed when a new field of grass is being sown.

The food web of a tawny owl. In real
life many more species are involved than
are shown here.

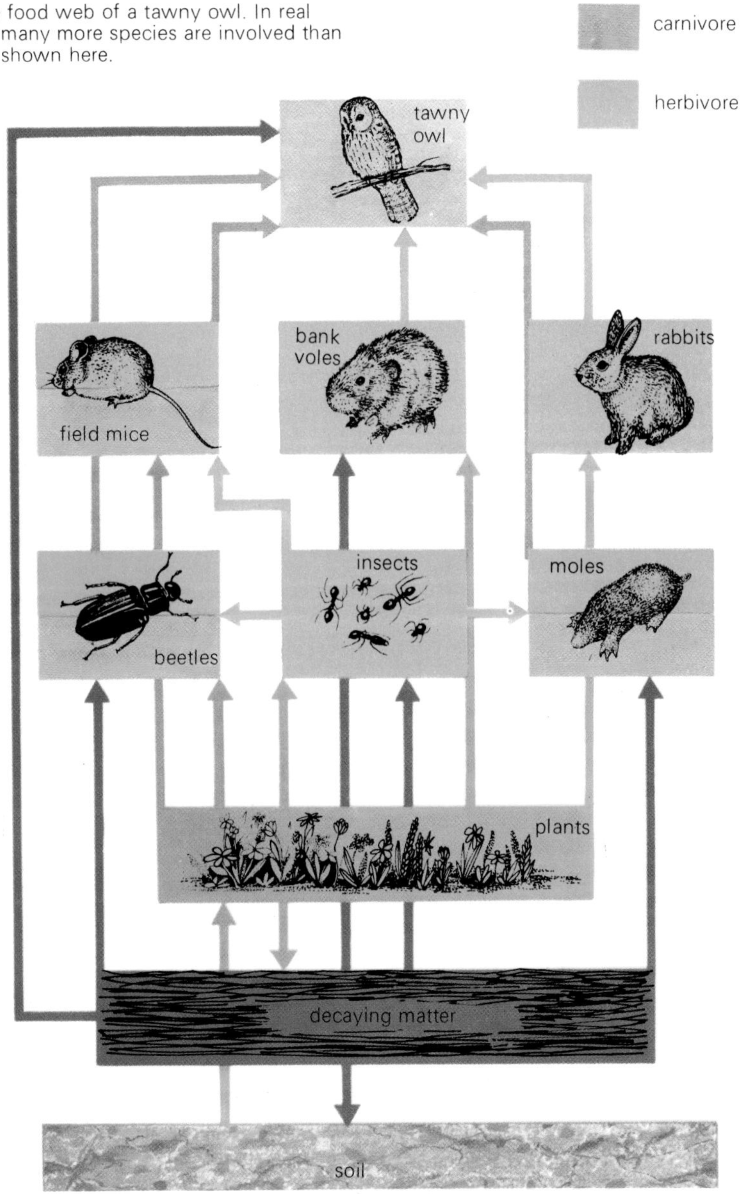

carnivore

herbivore

tawny
owl

bank
voles

rabbits

field mice

insects

moles

beetles

plants

decaying matter

soil

Seed-eating birds, such as finches, will be attracted to meadows, and so will birds like starlings that winkle out grubs and other such creatures from just below the surface. Small mammals feed on the seeds, too. Mice and voles are common in grasslands and although not often seen themselves, the runs they make through the grass tussocks can be found quite easily.

Owls and weasels will hunt for these small rodents, so obviously there will be food chains and webs to discover in the meadows, just as there were in the woods.

Insects abound in meadows. Grasshoppers, crickets, butterflies, moths, bugs and beetles are all very common. Adults are usually easy to find, but the other stages are more difficult.

Most insects start life as eggs. In some species, such as grasshoppers, the eggs hatch into *nymphs*, which are similar to adults but smaller and with tiny wings. The nymph moults several times as it grows and each time the wings get larger until finally the adult stage is reached.

Other insects, such as butterflies and beetles, hatch from the egg as a *larva* which looks nothing like the adult. Later, the larva becomes a *pupa*. In this stage it rests while great changes take place inside it. From the pupa, the adult emerges to move about, mate, and lay more eggs.

The hedge round the meadow is similar to a long, thin wood. The trees and shrubs in it provide shelter

The life history of a butterfly. A larva hatches from the egg and this develops into a pupa. Finally the adult emerges.

and nesting sites for many species of birds. Some will nest low down in the hedge while others prefer to nest higher.

Small mammals such as weasels and stoats, use the hedge for shelter. For many animals, the hedge makes good cover when moving long distances. This allows them to avoid being too long in the open where they might be caught by a larger predator. And, of course, the bank at the bottom of the hedge is just the place to look for basking lizards and snakes on sunny days.

Things to look for in Meadows & Hedges

Trees & Shrubs

Wych elm
Ulmus glabra
Up to about 40 metres high. Trunk often divides into two or three large branches low down. Leaves large, 80–160mm long, with the parts on each side of the main vein slightly different lengths, making leaves look lop-sided. Most kinds of elm send up suckers from roots, but not wych elms. Seeds have wings all round them.

Black poplar
Populus nigra
Height up to 30 metres. Variety best known is Lombardy poplar, so-called because it was first noticed in Italy. Easy to recognise because of its slender shape. Trunk very upright and each twig grows upright also. Leaves diamond-shaped. Often grown near the riverside, but not always.

Hawthorn
Crataegus monogyna
Shrub or small tree, 2–10 metres high. Twigs smooth. Thorny. Leaves small with lobed edges. Flowers usually in bunches. Petals white, sometimes pink. Fruit crimson, fleshy, with one hard stone inside. In Britain, sometimes called May tree, because that is the month it flowers.

Blackthorn
Prunus spinosa
Much-branched bush with very dark twigs. Thorny. Leaves 20–40mm long, oval. Flowers single, opening before leaves. Petals white; bush may be so full of blossom that it looks snow-covered. Fruit, called sloes, are like small, blue-black plums with a waxy powder on the surface. Very acid to the taste, but sometimes made into jelly or wine.

Dog rose
Rosa canina
Shrub 1–3 metres high. Branches arch over and carry many curved thorns. Leaves made up of leaflets, up to seven, attached to a main stalk. Flowers about 50mm across, five petals, pink, very delicate-looking. Fruit, called hips, are glossy, bright red, with many hairy seeds inside. Sometimes collected and made into jelly or syrup.

Herbs

Meadow-grass
Poa pratensis
Grows in tufts. Slender, creeping stems. Flowering stems 100–800mm tall, very slender with groups of very thin branches growing out from near the top. Each branch has small, flat group of flowers at the end, although as in all grasses they do not look like the usual idea of flowers since there are no coloured petals.

Meadow fox-tail
Alopecurus pratensis
Flowering stems up to 1 metre high. Flowers make a mass, about 60mm long, near upper end of stem. Each flower has a short, stiff hair which sticks out and these make the whole mass look like a hairy fox tail. A fairly easy grass to recognise.

Rye-grass
Lolium perenne
Smooth leaves, in tufts. Flowering stems wiry, 250–800mm tall. Groups of flowers small, flattened, eight to twenty of them growing in rows on

either side of stem, edge on to it. If flowers have hairs sticking up from them, the species is Italian rye-grass. Rye-grass is very common and often sown in leys.

Cocksfoot
Dactylis glomerata
A coarse grass that grows in tufts. Leaves rough. Flowering stems up to 1 metre high; thin, stiff, with short branches near the top. Flowers in tight groups at the end and each group is supposed to have the shape of a cock's foot, which is why it has this name. Found also by roadsides.

Buttercup
Ranunculus acris
Very common plant with hairy stem that branches a great deal. 150mm— 1 metre high. Leaves are hairy and have two to seven lobes. Each lobe has edges with large teeth. Leaves near base of plant have long stalks, but those higher up have shorter stalks or even none. Flowers golden yellow, 18—25mm across, petals rather rounded and very glossy. Not found in Portugal or southern Italy.

Cat's ear
Hypochaeris radicata
Common plant with leaves that grow as a rosette on the ground. Leaves 70—250mm long, hairy, with large teeth along edges. Stem 200—600mm tall, with a few branches. Flower heads made up of many small, golden yellow flowers looking like strap-shaped petals. Heads about 25—40mm across. Seeds have many silky hairs which help them to be carried off by the wind.

Daisy
Bellis perennis
Low growing, with leaves making a rosette on the ground and flower stems growing up from the centre of the rosette. Leaves spoon-shaped, edges bluntly toothed. 'Flower' is

really a mass of much smaller flowers, those in the centre forming a yellow mound, and those around the outside looking like white petals, sometimes tipped with pink.

Hedge parsley
Torilis japonica
Upright plant, up to 1·25 metres high. Stems stiff, hairy and ridged. Leaves long and made up of several pairs of notched leaflets on a central stalk, giving them a fern-like appearance. Flowers small, 2—3mm across, white or pink, each with five petals. Large numbers in bunches at the end of stalks which join the main stem at the same point. Found in hedges where it is abundant.

Yarrow
Achillea millefolium
Strongly scented plant with upright, downy stems, up to 450mm tall. Leaves fairly narrow; dark green, with a feathery appearance. Each flower head about 6mm across, and large numbers bunched together in white, flattish clusters. Used as a medicine in the past over much of Europe, and still used in Austria and Switzerland.

Hedge garlic
Alliaria petiolata
Upright stem. 200mm—1·2m, fairly smooth. Some leaves make a rosette against the ground. Those on stem are heart-shaped with toothed edges and smell of garlic when crushed. Flowers 6mm across, with four petals, white. Fruit are long, narrow pods. Found in hedges, edges of woods and shady gardens. Also called garlic mustard and Jack-by-the-hedge.

Ribwort plantain
Plantago lanceolata
One of the commonest European plants. Leaves 100—150mm long, narrowly oval with pointed tips and three to five ribs showing clearly. Flower stems furrowed. Flowers

small, dark brown, massed together as a short, finger-shaped knob at the end of stem. Ring of white *stamens* may be showing. These are the parts of the plant that produce pollen.

Field thistle
Cirsium arvense
Fairly tall, 300–900mm, with upright, tough stem, not winged. Leaves long, with sharp spines along edges and at the end. Flower heads like small purplish brushes, the lower part surrounded by vase-like coat of prickly scales called *bracts*. There are many species of thistle. That illustrated on page 63 is *Cirsium palustre* which is more likely to be found in wetter meadows and marshes. It can be recognised by the winged stems.

White clover
Trifolium repens
Creeping stems, which root where leaves join them. Leaves made up of three oval, almost round, leaflets usually with a whitish mark on them. Leaf stems up to 140mm. Each flower small, rather tubular, white. Many flowers massed into ball-shaped head. As they die and turn brown, they droop.

Dandelion
Taraxacum officinale
Low growing plant. Leaves vary in size but usually have large teeth along edges. Flower stems smooth and when broken ooze whitish 'milk'. Heads, 35–50mm across, of many strap-shaped, golden-yellow flowers. Below them are many green bracts Each seed is attached to a 'parachute' and all of them in the head make a ball-shaped mass which is easily scattered by the wind.

Bird's-foot trefoil
Lotus corniculatus
Stems lie on ground, 100–400mm long. Leaves with five oval leaflets, but lowest pair bend back so there appear to be only three. Two to six flowers bunched at top of stem, each like a pea or bean flower, yellow tinged with red. Seeds contained in a pod. Sometimes this is called 'bacon and eggs'.

Birds

Partridge
Perdix perdix
Length 300mm. Widespread throughout most of Europe, except northern Scandinavia and much of Spain. Very common on any kind of open land. Mainly brown and grey, with chestnut-coloured face, neck and tail. Chestnut bands on sides and patch on breast. When startled, flies up with noisy wing-beats. Red-legged partridge similar and found in England, France and Spain.

Pheasant
Phasianus colchicus
Length, male 840mm, female 580mm. Male mainly copper-coloured with white collar, glossy green head and red eye-patch. Female duller, mottled brown. Both male and female have long tail feathers. Mainly a ground-living bird, eating grain, seeds and berries. If startled will fly up with a noisy, whirring sound, but will not fly very far.

Skylark
Alauda arvensis
Length 180mm. Common in meadowland and usually noticed when singing high in the air during the first half of the year. Brown, with streaky appearance on back. Underparts light; breast speckled. Light stripe over eyes and small crest on head. Nests on ground, cup-shaped and made of grass lined with hair. May be seen in flocks after the breeding season is over.

Swallow
Hirundo rustica

Length 190mm. Dark blue upper parts, red throat and chest, forked tail with long outer feathers like streamers. Very graceful flight and very fast in order to catch insects on the wing. Sometimes may be seen flying close to surface of lakes and canals. Nest made of mud, fixed to ledge of farm building. Migrates to Africa during winter months.

Carrion crow
Corvus corone corone

Length 460mm. About same size as rook. Very similar in appearance but without pale skin at base of beak. More often seen in ones and twos, although family groups are common in summer. Eats carrion, eggs, nestling birds, as well as grain and fruit. Pairs nest separately rather than in groups as rooks. Not found in Italy or Scandinavia.

Jackdaw
Corvus monedula

Length 330mm. Almost completely black but with grey neck and sides of face. Common around farms and will sometimes pluck wool from sheeps' backs for lining nests. Will eat almost anything, but eats large quantities of grain and insects. May mix with rooks and starlings. Call is a very sharp 'jack', often repeated over and over again.

Rook
Corvus frugilegus

Length 460mm. Large, all-black bird, very similar to carrion crow but has white skin around base of beak and is more often seen in flocks. Found over most of Europe in summer, but leaves northern countries in winter when ground becomes frozen. Nests in treetop 'rookeries' sometimes containing dozens of nests, occasionally hundreds.

Corn bunting
Emberiza calandra

Length 180mm. Dull-coloured bird, brown with streaky appearance. Short, stout beak, typical of seed-eating birds. In summer, males may sit on posts or wires, singing for long periods, but the song is rather dull and sounds like a bunch of keys being jangled. When breeding season is finished, corn buntings may flock with other kinds of buntings and finches.

Song thrush
Turdus philomelos

Length 230mm. Plain brown above, spotted below. Usually seen alone. Feeds on snails, worms, insects, fruit and seeds. Breaks snail shells by banging them on a particular stone called the 'anvil', which will have broken shells around it. Mistle thrush looks similar but is larger. Neither found in northern Scandinavia.

Fieldfare
Turdus pilaris

Length 250mm. One of the larger thrushes.Often seen in mixed flocks with redwings. Brown back, darker tail. Spotted underside. Grey head and rump. Breeds in Scandinavia but migrates southwards in winter when it can be seen in Britain, usually on stubble but occasionally in gardens. Also called the blueback.

Redwing
Turdus iliacus

Length 200mm. A small thrush, recognised by the white stripe above the eyes and red patches under wings which make the bird look as if it may be injured on its side. Breeds in northern countries but migrates southwards during the winter. It can be seen in Britain, often in mixed flocks with fieldfares, feeding in open fields and sometimes in gardens, but then only in ones or twos.

Goldfinch
Carduelis carduelis
Length 120mm. Male very attractive with red face and golden yellow bars on wings. Rest of body quite strongly patterned in white, black and pale brown. Female similar, also with golden wing bars, but with less red on face. Often seen in flocks, especially on patches of seeding thistles.

Dunnock
Prunella modularis
Length 150mm. Small bird, striped brown back, grey head and breast. Narrow, pointed beak. Often called hedge sparrow but is not a true sparrow, getting the name only because years ago any small bird was called a sparrow by countrymen. Feeds on ground. Nests in low bushes and hedges, and is a common victim of cuckoos.

Yellowhammer
Emberiza citrinella
Length 160mm. Common in open country with bushes and hedges. Males have reddish-brown wings, back and tail, with large amount of bright yellow on head and underparts. Females less colourful. A seed-eater with fairly short, stout beak. Nests on ground or bank, sometimes even on a wall, but not high up. Song supposed to sound like 'little bit of bread and no cheese'.

Chaffinch
Fringilla coelebs
Length 150mm. One of the most common birds of Europe, although town-people might find this hard to believe. Males are colourful, with blue-grey head and neck, pink breast and cheeks, white bars on wings and white sides of tail. Females less colourful, yellowish-brown above and creamy-brown below. Outside the breeding season, chaffinches may be seen in flocks of thousands.

Little owl
Athene noctua
Length 220mm. Common across Europe, but not found in Scandinavia. Greyish-brown and white, speckled. Rather squat appearance and rather large head which is slightly flattened and makes the bird look as if it is scowling. Often seen in daylight perching on fences or telegraph wires. Bobs its body when nervous. Eats small mammals, young birds and large numbers of insects.

Barn owl
Tyto alba
Length 350mm. Common around farmland. Golden brown, speckled upper parts; white face and underparts. Fawn-breasted form of barn owl may be seen in eastern and southern Europe. Heart-shaped face. Shrieking cry has given it the name of screech owl in some places. Hunts voles, mice, etc., mainly by hearing. Not found in Scandinavia.

Mammals

Common vole
Microtus arvalis
Small mammal, body length 95—120mm. Has a smooth appearance. More rounded head than field mouse and smaller ears. Active mainly at dusk, although it moves about also during the night and daytime, but it has long periods of rest. Makes short tunnels with store-rooms and also nest-rooms. Not found in Britain except as rare forms in the Orkneys and Guernsey.

Harvest mouse
Micromys minutus
Europe's smallest rodent. Body length 58—76mm, tail 51—72mm. Lives in cornfields and rough grassland where it can get food and shelter and make its ball-shaped nest which it weaves

among the plant-stems. Not found in Spain, Scandinavia or high mountain regions.

Field mouse
Apodemus sylvaticus
Sometimes called wood mouse, although it lives mainly in open country rather than in woods. Body length 77–110mm with a long tail that may be longer than the body. Large ears and large, black eyes. Underside white. Yellow-necked mouse similar, but with yellow band across throat. Active mainly at night. Found all over Europe except northern Scandinavia.

Mole
Talpa europaea
Burrowing mammal. Body length 115–150mm. Short tail. Long snout and almost no neck. Ears and eyes hidden by soft, thick, black fur. Front legs short, feet broad, turned out and with long claws. Back feet smaller. Found over most of Europe except Ireland, western Spain and the greater part of Scandinavia.

Rabbit
Oryctolagus cuniculus
Body length 340–455mm. Very small tail. Long ears, but not as long as those of hare. Powerful hind legs and long hind feet. Upper parts grey, light underneath, but in southern France there are some black ones. Live in system of burrows called warrens, but come to surface to graze on grass and other small plants. Not found in high mountains and absent from much of Italy and Scandinavia.

Brown hare
Lepus capensis
Similar shape to rabbit but larger. Ears longer with black tips. Front legs long. Tail black on upper side. Does not live in groups and does not burrow. Mediterranean race is smaller and has black on the upper sides of neck and back, giving animal a

speckled appearance. Rests in a depression in the ground which is called a *form*.

Stoat
Mustela erminea
Similar shape to weasel, but much larger. Body length 220–290mm, tail 80–120mm *with black tip*. That, and larger size are the best way to distinguish stoat from weasel. In some countries, stoats turn white in winter, but tip of tail still remains black. Able to kill mammals up to the size of rabbits for food. Not found in southern Europe.

Weasel
Mustela nivalis
The smallest European carnivore. Body length of male 210–230mm, females much smaller. Tail 60–65mm, without black tip. Long, narrow body, brown above and white below. Weasels hunt mainly at night, but it is not uncommon to see them during the day. They feed on small mammals such as mice and voles.

Hedgehog
Erinaceus europeus
Length up to 275mm. Plump body with high, rounded back. Small head with pointed snout and bright, black eyes. Small, rounded ears. Top of head and upper parts of body covered with stiff, sharp-pointed spines about 25mm long. Rest of body covered in coarse, grey-brown hair. Active mainly at dusk, snuffling as it searches for beetles, slugs, etc. to eat. Rolls up into a ball when in danger. Also comes into gardens where it can be encouraged by leaving bowls of bread and milk of which it is very fond.

Cattle
Kept on farms all over Europe, some for fattening as beef, others for milk. Beef cattle tend to be heavier in appearance. Some breeds are horned,

others hornless. Cattle chew the cud: they eat grass which is swallowed and partly digested. Later in the day, it is brought back to the mouth for a second chewing before swallowing again and digesting completely. There are many breeds, common ones being Hereford, Simmental, Charolais, Jersey and Friesian.

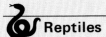

Reptiles

Green lizard
Lacerta viridis
Length up to 500mm. Central and southern Europe, not in Britain. Bright green with long tail, twice as long as body; tail breaks off easily.

Seen in dry places sunning itself but will hide under stones at slightest hint of danger. A very handsome reptile.

Common lizard
Lacerta vivipara
Length 150mm but half of this is tail. Colour varies but is usually grey or brown with rows of paler spots on back. Very common and hardy. Found farther north than any other European lizard. Often seen sunning itself on hedgebanks, but darts away when disturbed. Most lizards lay eggs, but the young of the common lizard are born alive.

Slow-worm
Anguis fragilis
Length up to 360mm. A legless lizard which looks like a snake, but has a lizard-like head, ear openings and eyelids, which snakes do not have. Body covered with tightly-fitting, brownish, glossy scales which make the animal look smooth and varnished. Some slow-worms are spotted with blue. They live along hedgerows, around the edges of woods and are also quite often found in churchyards.

Invertebrates

Large copper
Lycaena dispar
There are many species of copper butterflies. The large copper is found in marshy fields, although not in Britain where it is now extinct. Other, smaller species will be seen all over Europe and can be recognised by the fiery copper colour of the wings. The larvae feed on various species of dock leaves.

Orange tip
Anthocharis cardamines
Wingspan nearly 40mm. Fore-wings are white with dark markings at the edges, but the most useful mark for recognition of male is the large orange patch. Hind wings are mottled greenish on upper and lower surfaces. Common in meadows, especially near hedges. Larvae feed on plants such as hedge mustard and garlic mustard.

Large skipper
Ochlodes venata
Wingspan about 30mm. A small butterfly, despite its name, very common in open spaces. Wings reddish-brown, much duller near edges, with yellowish spots near dark border. Males have black, slanting streak in middle of front wings. No dark streak in females. Underside of wings paler and females have yellow on front pair of wings and pale green on hind pair. Larvae feed on grasses.

Cinnabar
Callimorpha jacobaeae
A small moth, about 40mm wingspan. Fore-wings black with red stripe and two red spots. Hind wings red with black edges. Black and red are 'warning colours' which discourage birds from eating the moth, which probably has an unpleasant taste. Burnet moths are also red and

black. They may be seen in meadows flying during the day. Most moths are night-flying.

Common blue
Polyommatus icarus
There are several species of blues and it is the common blue that is most likely to be seen in large numbers in meadows. Upper surface of wings blue with white margins. Females have small orange and black markings near edges also. Underside bluish-grey or fawn with many dark spots ringed with white, and orange patches near edges. The large blue is very rare in Britain, but more plentiful over much of Europe.

Cranefly
Tipula paludosa
Sometimes called daddy-long-legs. Thin grey-brown body and very thin, extremely long legs which break off easily. One pair of wings, which in some species may have a span of over 60mm. Other species have smaller wings. Larva lives in soil or in decaying wood or leaf litter.

Soldier beetle
Cantharis fusca
A fairly small beetle, about 10mm long, with an oblong shape and rather soft wing-cases. Reddish body and black wing-cases. Often found clinging to grass stems and flowers of meadow plants. Several different, but related, beetles are given the name of soldier beetles. Because of their red colour, they are often called 'bloodsuckers', but they are quite harmless. They visit flowers to catch other, smaller insects.

Burying beetle
Necrophorus vespilloides
Also called sexton beetle. Stout body, 25mm long. Black with orange bands on wing-cases. Good sense of smell and is attracted to small, dead mammals and birds. A pair of beetles will bury one of these by digging out soil from under it. The female then lays her eggs close to it so that the dead animal becomes food for the beetle larvae when they hatch.

Green grasshopper
Omacestus viridulus
Length about 20mm. Common in Britain and over most of Europe but not in far south. Found in grassy places and heard throughout the summer, but hard to see because of its green and brown colour, and difficult to catch. Many species of grasshopper and cricket are likely to be found in meadows.

Field cricket
Gryllus campestris
Length up to 25mm. Stout body. Wings lying flatter on the back than in grasshoppers, and shorter. Two hairy 'tails' at hind end of body and also the egg-laying tube in females. Much darker and greyer than grasshoppers. Noisy. Song made by rubbing wings together.

Harvestman
Opilio paretinus
Related to spiders. Eight very long, slender legs, but a very small body less than 10mm long. Also nicknamed daddy-long-legs in same way as cranefly which may be confusing. Harvestmen feed on insects, millipedes or small worms, but they may also eat some plant material. Eggs are laid under logs and stones. Many species.

Brown-lipped snail
Cepaea nemoralis
Common snail of hedgerows. Shell about 20mm broad, yellowish colour but pink ones also common; brown lip and brown spiral bands, any number up to five. Colour pattern of this snail varies. Some give better protection in hedges, others are better in woods, or in grass.

 # Trees & Shrubs

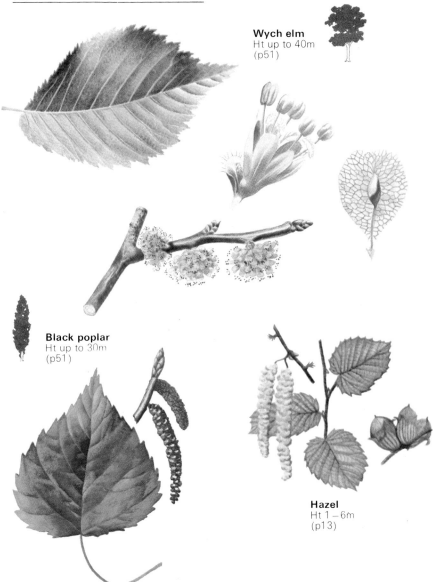

Wych elm
Ht up to 40m
(p51)

Black poplar
Ht up to 30m
(p51)

Hazel
Ht 1 – 6m
(p13)

Hawthorn
Ht 2 – 10m
(p51)

Blackthorn
Ht 1 – 4m
(p51)

Dog rose
Ht 1 – 3m
(p51)

Herbs

Meadow-grass
Ht 100 – 800mm
(p51)

Cocksfoot
Ht up to 1m
(p52)

Meadow fox-tail
Ht up to 1m
(p51)

Buttercup
Ht 150mm – 1m
(p52)

Rye-grass
Ht 250 – 800mm
(p51)

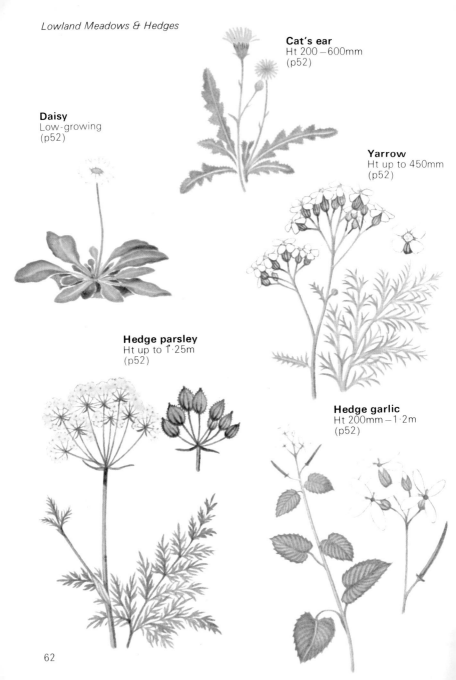

Cat's ear
Ht 200 – 600mm
(p52)

Daisy
Low-growing
(p52)

Yarrow
Ht up to 450mm
(p52)

Hedge parsley
Ht up to 1·25m
(p52)

Hedge garlic
Ht 200mm – 1·2m
(p52)

Ribwort plantain
Low-growing
(p52)

White clover
Creeping
(p53)

Dandelion
Low-growing
(p53)

Field thistle
Ht 300 – 900mm
(p53)

Bird's-foot trefoil
Creeping (L 100 – 400mm)
(p53)

Birds

Skylark
L 180mm
(p53)

Partridge
L 300mm
(p53)

Pheasant
L (m) 840mm; (f) 580mm
(p53)

Swallow
L 190mm
(p54)

Carrion crow
L 460mm
(p54)

Rook
L 460mm
(p54)

Jackdaw
L 330mm
(p54)

Corn bunting
L 180mm
(p54)

Song thrush
L 230mm
(p54)

Goldcrest
L 90mm
(p18)

Fieldfare
L 250mm
(p54)

Redwing
L 200mm
(p54)

Chaffinch
L 150mm
(p55)

Goldfinch
L 120mm
(p55)

Yellowhammer
L 160mm
(p55)

Dunnock
L 150mm
(p55)

Little owl
L 220mm
(p55)

Barn owl
L 350mm
(p55)

Mammals

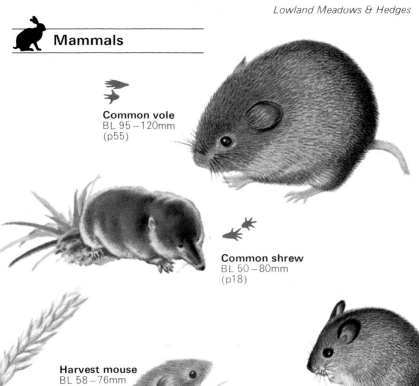

Common vole
BL 95 – 120mm
(p55)

Common shrew
BL 50 – 80mm
(p18)

Harvest mouse
BL 58 – 76mm
(p55)

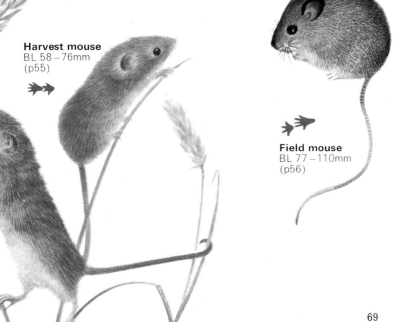

Field mouse
BL 77 – 110mm
(p56)

Mole
BL 115   150mm
(p56)

Stoat
BL 220 – 290mm
(p56)

Rabbit
BL 340 – 455mm
(p56)

Weasel
BL 210 – 230mm
(p56)

Brown hare
BL 485 – 675mm
(p56)

Hedgehog
BL 225 – 275mm
(p56)

Hereford
(p56)

Friesian
(p56)

Simmental
(p56)

Jersey
(p56)

Charolais
(p56)

 **Reptiles**

Green lizard
L up to 500mm
(p57)

Common lizard
L up to 150mm
(p57)

Slow-worm
L up to 360mm
(p57)

Invertebrates

Large copper
Ws 40mm
(p57)

Large skipper
Ws 30mm
(p57)

Orange tip
Ws 40mm
(p57)

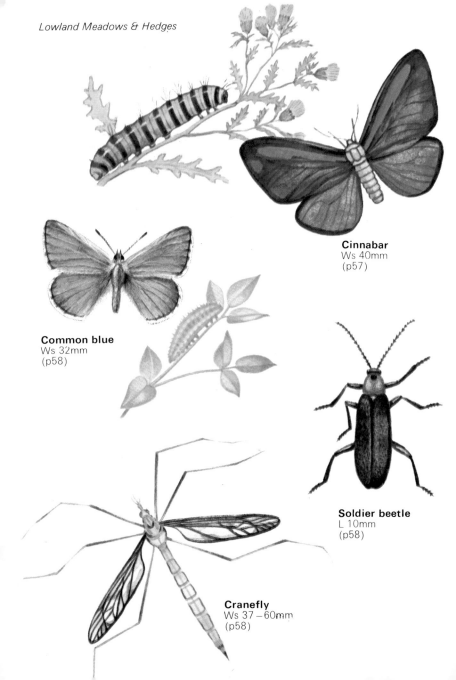

Cinnabar
Ws 40mm
(p57)

Common blue
Ws 32mm
(p58)

Soldier beetle
L 10mm
(p58)

Cranefly
Ws 37 –60mm
(p58)

Burying beetle
L 25mm
(p58)

Field cricket
L 25mm
(p58)

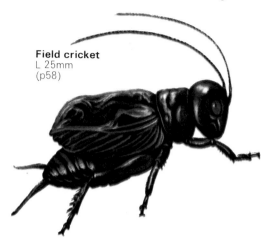

Green grasshopper
L 20mm
(p58)

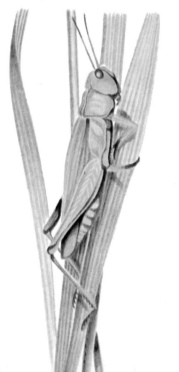

Harvestman
BL up to 10mm
(p58)

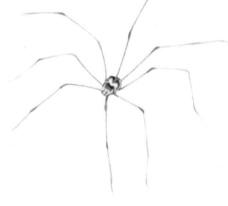

Brown-lipped snail
Shell up to 20mm wide
(p58)

Rivers, Streams & Ponds

Many rivers start high up in the mountains where rain or water from melting snows form rivulets running down the slope. These join to make a small and fast-running stream; the steeper the slope, the faster the water will rush along. Several streams may join up and make a larger river which continues on its downward course. Lower down, the slope will become gentler and the river slows and widens.

The water is on its way to the sea and when it reaches the flatter ground, the river grows more sluggish and begins to twist and turn as it finds the easiest course to take. The speed and power that it had when it began made it possible for the river to cut a channel that was

We must all keep an eye on pollution if we want to see life flourishing in rivers.

almost straight. Near its end in the sea, the speed and power have gone.

Other rivers begin life as springs where water rises up from below the surface of the ground; the journey to the sea is much the same as for the first type of river except, of course, that unless the spring is on a steep slope, the current at the beginning will not be a fast one.

As the river flows from its source to the mouth, it affects the ground

Below: a youthful river. At this stage waterfalls, cascades and small lakes abound.

over which it travels. The fast mountain torrent wears away the rock and cuts a channel down into it. The pieces of broken rock can be carried by the water and will break up still further into sand grains and small pebbles. Larger pebbles may be rolled over and over on the river bed. A fast-running mountain torrent can carry a large load of rock

Above: a mature river. By now the valley has widened, the current is slackening and sand and stone are beginning to collect on the river bed.

Left: a senile river. It is now quite wide and flowing slowly, as it twists and turns on its course to the sea.

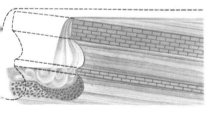

Above: waterfalls are caused by resistant rock. The dotted lines show the original position of the rock, indicating how the fall has been cut back.

fragments weighing several tonnes.

As the current slackens, some of the load is dropped. Sand and stones begin to collect on the river bed, especially near the banks where the river turns.

Meanwhile the river can still continue slowly to cut away its banks. The mud made can be carried until it meets the sea water in the estuary and then it, too, is dropped to pile up as mud banks.

So during its journey, a river will be wearing away, or *eroding*, rocks. It will be carrying particles, and it will be dropping, or *depositing*, a great deal of material as well.

In limestone regions, a river may behave in a slightly different way by disappearing down a crack or hole. Then it will continue on its way underground, following the downward slope towards the sea. The water will dissolve some of the limestone, however, and form underground caves, some of which may be very large.

Canals are man-made and are like slow-running rivers, but because the water will only flow when lock-gates are opened, for long periods it will be still. Then the canals behave as a series of very long ponds.

The water of ponds is almost always very still and this gives many plants a chance to grow. This, in turn, enables many animals to live and breed there, provided the water does not grow too stagnant and stale. If this happens the amount of life in the pond will fall to almost nothing.

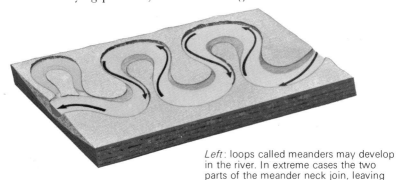

Left: loops called meanders may develop in the river. In extreme cases the two parts of the meander neck join, leaving an ox-bow lake.

79

Life in Rivers, Streams & Ponds

All food chains begin with plants and those in ponds are no exception, but to the thousands of small, fresh-water animals, the important plants are not the large ones by the bank, but the microscopic ones in the water. Bacteria and algae are food for the small animals which can just be seen with the naked eye, the water-fleas and others about the same size. In the early summer, there may be so many water-fleas that small fish and newts can gorge themselves. But these, in turn, will fall prey to the larger fish, or birds such as the kingfishers and herons that end the food chain.

Other pond creatures are scavengers and eat the rotting remains of the various plants and animals, large or small, that fall to the bottom of the pond, while some, such as the pond-skaters, walk on the surface of the pond ready to eat any small insect that may fall onto the water.

The food webs of ponds and rivers can be very complicated and if you wish to try and work some out, you will need to watch carefully by the pond side, and also possibly keep some of the creatures in aquaria.

Fresh-water plants need water, light and oxygen just as land plants do and a fresh-water habitat has some advantages over a land one. At least there is usually no shortage of water! However, conditions around a pond do vary tremendously from place to place and each kind of plant is adapted for living with its roots in a particular amount of water.

Every pond plant is likely to fall into one of five groups. Firstly there are those that float on the surface of the water with no roots to attach them to the bottom. Duckweed and water fern are in this group.

The second group contains those plants that go to the other extreme and are completely submerged and often rooted in the mud. Hornwort

and water milfoil are plants of this type. In fact, hornwort not only grows under the water (although not actually rooted), but flowers there too, the pollen being carried

A food chain in which microscopic plants are eaten by shrimps. These are then eaten by fish which in turn fall prey to the heron.

from one flower to another by the water.

In the third group are the water-lilies, water soldier, water crow-foot and the many others that are rooted in the mud at the bottom of the pond but grow up to the surface. Although some leaves may be submerged, others lie on the surface along with the flowers.

Group four includes all those plants of the pond and river's edge that prefer swampy conditions. The greater part of these plants stand up above the water, and they are the ones most noticeable when walk-by the pond or along the canal bank. Yellow iris, water forget-me-not, purple loosestrife, as well as the reedmace and sweet flag, grow in these swampy conditions.

Finally, there are the plants (such as the great willow-herb and the meadowsweet) that like the damp, but not wet, soil that is a little farther from the water's edge.

The plants of the last two groups sometimes vary in their position, so it is sometimes easier to put them together and call them the group of waterside plants.

Animals living in the water are well-adapted for living there. Those of fast running streams must not be swept away and so many have flat bodies for hiding under stones, or possibly some particular way of clinging tightly to the stones or weeds instead.

Water animals may have different methods of feeding from land-living ones. Many are filter-feeders, strain-ing tiny particles of food from the water in the way the water-fleas or the mussels do. Some species of caddis larvae spin nets in order to trap food as water flows through them. Of course there are herbivores and carnivores too, just as there are on land.

Breathing under water is different from breathing on land. Some animals overcome the problem by having a thin tube which can be pushed to the surface and used for taking in air. Others collect a film or bubble of air at the surface and take it down with them. Many water beetles obtain their oxygen in this way and so does the water spider, which actually collects the air bubbles under a silken web as they are taken down, making a kind of diving bell.

Many fresh-water inhabitants can absorb oxygen from the water by using gills. Fish, of course, have gills, but so also do mayfly and dragonfly nymphs. Some simply absorb the oxygen through their skin.

The life histories of many fresh-water animals are interesting. That of the mosquito is much like that of many insects. Eggs are laid on the surface of the water. They are joined together to make a small raft, only a few millimetres across. Larvae then hatch from these eggs. Mos-quito larvae hang head-down in the water, with a breathing-tube reach-ing to the surface. They filter food

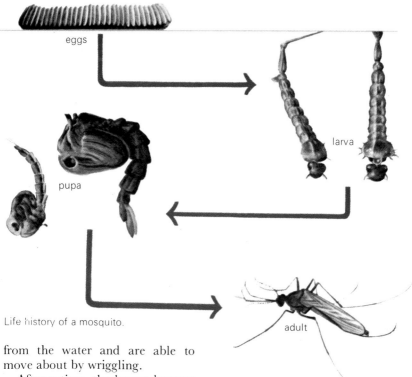

eggs

larva

pupa

adult

Life history of a mosquito.

from the water and are able to move about by wriggling.

After a time, the larvae become pupae, the resting and changing stage. These pupae look a little like large commas, with the head close to the surface. When the changes have been completed inside each pupa, the skin splits and the adult mosquito pulls itself out.

Dragonflies have a slightly different life history. The eggs are laid singly in the water and each one hatches into a nymph. This looks very little like a dragonfly. It is a carnivore and crawls around among the pond plants catching other small creatures to eat. After a long period,

maybe a year or two, the nymph will climb up a stem and out of the water. Its skin will split and the adult dragonfly will emerge, to unfold its crumpled wings and fly off.

The life history of frogs is very different. Frogs' eggs are laid in water, each one a tiny, black ball surrounded by jelly and many of them sticking together to form a mass called frog spawn. Each black ball develops a tail as it grows and finally it breaks out of the jelly to swim around as a tadpole.

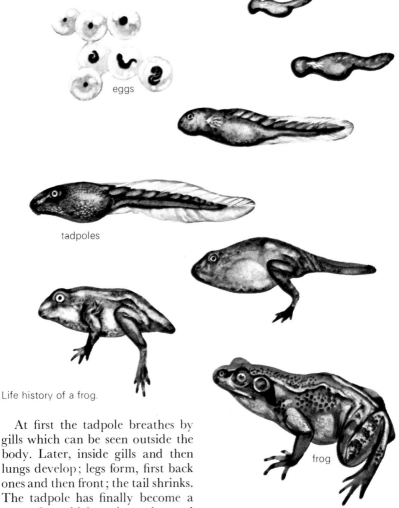

eggs

tadpoles

Life history of a frog.

frog

At first the tadpole breathes by gills which can be seen outside the body. Later, inside gills and then lungs develop; legs form, first back ones and then front; the tail shrinks. The tadpole has finally become a young frog which can leave the pond although it will take several years to grow to its full size when it will be able to breed.

Fish and birds are very much a part of fresh-water life too, playing their parts as steps in food chains. Large ones like the pike and heron will be at the end of the chain, but the smaller fish and young birds will be somewhere in the middle.

Things to look for in Rivers, Streams & Ponds

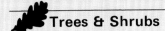

Trees & Shrubs

Alder
Alnus glutinosa
Tree of wet places, up to 20 metres high. Bark dark brown and grooved. Buds have short stalk. Leaves dark green and almost circular but with a wide notch at the end so that some are almost heart-shaped; toothed edges. Male catkins long and narrow with reddish appearance when young. Female catkins much shorter and rounder; can be seen on tree in winter looking like small, black pine cones.

White willow
Salix alba
Height 10–20 metres. Greyish bark with deep furrows in it. Leaves long, 50–100mm, narrow and pointed with slightly toothed edges, greyish-green above and silvery-white below. When tree is rustled by wind, it has a rather whitish appearance. This is the reason for its name. Catkins are white and look furry. Branches sometimes deliberately cut back and allowed to grow again from top of trunk. This is called *pollarding*. It is one of the fastest growing of all trees.

Goat willow
Salix caprea
Shrub or small tree, 3–10 metres high. Leaves oval with veins showing clearly. Catkins white and furry-looking, showing before leaves grow. Often picked for decoration. Called goat willow because leaves were once used as food for goats. Does not need such damp ground as other willows and is often found in hedges and scrubland, as well as near streams and ponds.

Herbs

Duckweed
Lemna minor
Very small floating plant with several 'leaves' joined together, each one about 4mm across or less. Root hanging down into water. May have tiny flowers that may not be noticed. Sometimes so plentiful that whole surface of water is covered. Several different species but all small.

Water milfoil
Myriophyllum spicatum
Submerged water plant, with creeping rootstock in mud. Stem 0·5–2·5 metres long, but lower part usually has no leaves because older ones have dropped off. Leaves in fours, divided into many fine segments giving feathery appearance. Flowers separate male and female, in small groups on stalks which grow above water; small, dull red. Found in ditches and ponds.

Water crowfoot
Ranunculus aquatilis
A member of the buttercup family which grows in ponds, streams and ditches throughout Europe. Stems submerged and branched. Underwater leaves very divided and feathery, 30–60mm long. Floating leaves deeply cut into segments. Flowers white with yellow centre, 10–20mm across, similar in shape to meadow buttercup; five petals. Fruit small and clustered in spiky ball at top of stem.

Hornwort
Ceratophyllum demersum
Found in ponds and ditches. Whole plant below surface. No roots. Leaves dark green, rather stiff and forked,

thread-like, about 20mm long. A number of leaves grow out in all directions from same point on stem. Flowers small, male whitish and female green.

Water-lily
Nuphar lutea
Grows in lakes, canals and slow-running rivers. Rooted in mud at bottom, but leaves and flowers float on surface. Leaves large, oval, almost circular, up to 400mm across, with deep cut in base from edge to stem. Flowers of yellow water-lily like large buttercup, up to 60mm across, just above the water. That of white water-lily has many white petals, oval and slightly pointed. Up to 200mm across and floating.

Arrowhead
Sagittaria sagittifolia
Found in shallow ponds, canals and slow-running rivers with muddy bottoms. There are three kinds of leaves. Underwater ones long and narrow; floating ones more oval; those that grow up into the air are arrow-shaped, 50–200mm long. Flowers in several groups of two or three on upright stem, white with purple patch in centre, three petals.

Sweet flag
Acorus calamus
Stout plant, up to 1 metre, growing in shallow water at edge of ponds and canals. Leaves upright, 10–20mm wide, with pointed tip; edges crinkled. Sweet-smelling when crushed. Small, yellowish flowers packed into an upward-pointing spike. Introduced into Europe by 1557 and was once gathered to be used for covering floors of churches and halls.

Reedmace
Typha latifolia
Grows in large patches at edge of ponds and canals. Leaves tall, often

over 2 metres, and may be twisted; greyish and rough. Flowers packed into a soft, brown, sausage-shaped mass, 100–150mm high, at the end of a tall, upright, stiff stem. When seeds are ripe, the mass loosens and then is scattered by the wind. Also called bulrush and cat's-tail. Lesser reedmace is similar, but smaller.

Common reed
Phragmites australis
Stout, tall reed, up to 3 metres high, with narrow leaves that die down in winter. Flowers in graceful, nodding plumes, dull purple, at top of tall stems. Plumes remain all through winter, but become silvery-grey. Creeping, underground stems enable plant to spread quickly and easily in wet ground.

Bur-reed
Sparganium erectum
A sturdy, upright reed with a smooth stem, up to 1·25 metres high. Leaves upright, about 15mm wide and three-sided. Flowers green and grouped as spiky balls on branched stalks, male flowers above female. Very common along the edges of rivers and canals throughout Britain and northern Europe.

Iris
Iris pseudacorus
Also called yellow flag. Upright plant, 0·5–1·5 metres tall, growing in shallow water at edges of ponds and rivers, etc. Leaves strap-shaped, with pointed tip, lower ends wrapped around stem. Flowers large, yellow and showy, several grouped together. Outer petals hang down and are said to resemble flags, which is the reason for the name of yellow flag.

Great willow-herb
Epilobrium hirsutum
Tall plant of river and pond edges, up to 1·5 metres high. Stem upright and branched near top. Hairy. Leaves

opposite one another, oblong with a pointed end and toothed edges. Flowers purplish-pink, 15–23mm across. In centre of each is a thin *stigma* with four narrow lobes turned back. Seed-pod long and narrow, splitting when ripe to allow seeds to be blown off by wind. Also called codlins-and-cream.

Water forget-me-not
Myosotis scorpioides
Low growing plant of the water's edge. Stem may be upright or partly creeping, 150–450mm long, hairy and branched. Leaves long-oval with blunt point. Buds usually pink but flowers usually blue, although sometimes pink or white, 4–10mm across; flat. Flowers grow on one side of stem which coils round.

Purple loosestrife
Lythrum salicaria
Height 600–1·2 metres. Tall, upright, leafy plant of swampy ground. Stem with four angles, rather than rounded like most plants. Leaves fairly long, 40–70mm, but only about 15mm wide, narrowing to a pointed tip, many of them turning red later in summer. Flowers purplish-pink, 10–15mm across, 4–6 petals, with rather untidy appearance. Many flowers, tightly clustered along upper part of stem.

Meadowsweet
Filipendula ulmaria
Height 600–1·2 metres. A tall, very graceful plant, growing by streams and rivers, in marshes and wet meadows. Lower leaves 300–600mm long, made up of several pairs of leaflets with toothed edges and end leaflet with three lobes; dark green on upper surface but greyish-white beneath because of many small hairs. Flowers small, creamy-white, in dense clusters at end of stem, often drooping slightly.

 Birds

Grey heron
Ardea cinerea
Length 1 metre. Large, grey bird with long legs, often seen standing without movement in open water looking for fish. Long neck mainly white. Black crest and some black lines on neck and sides. Long pointed beak. Flies with slow wing beats, head and neck drawn back. Produces a powder among its breast feathers. Heron puts this on plumage when preening to remove slime from fish which may have got there when feeding.

Mallard
Anas platyrhyncos
Length 590mm. Most common of the surface-feeding ducks. Drake has glossy green head, white collar and reddish-brown breast. Duck is dull brown. Both have blue wing patch which does not always show when swimming. Flies well with neck outstretched. Found on lakes, ponds, rivers, marshes and along coast.

Great crested grebe
Podiceps cristatus
Length 450mm. Seen on lakes and large ponds with reeds at the edge. Brown with white throat and underparts. White face and dark streak through eye. Long, upright neck and fairly long beak. Easily recognised in spring and summer by tufts of red-brown feathers on side of head and dark brown tufts on top like ears. Dives a great deal and in breeding season has interesting courtship display.

Mute swan
Cygnus olor
Length 1·5 metres. Heavy, long-necked bird. Adult white; orange beak with black knob close to head. Young, called *cygnets*, are greyish-brown. When swimming, head and

neck held up and neck curved gracefully, but dipped into water when feeding on plants at bottom. Flies with neck outstretched and noisy wing-beats. May be seen on rivers, lakes, along seashore and in parks where it becomes semi-tame.

Dabchick
Podiceps ruficollis

Length 250mm. Also known as little grebe. Common on lakes and old gravel pits with plenty of vegetation. Dark brown with reddish-brown throat. Dives a great deal and swims under water for quite long distances, looking for fish and water insects to eat. Makes a floating nest and covers eggs with weed when nest is to be left for a while.

Coot
Fulica atra

Length 370mm. Similar to moorhen, but slightly larger and no white feathers. White beak and forehead patch. Very large feet and toes have lobes of skin along each side making feet partly webbed. Nest made among reeds. When taking off to fly, has to run along surface of water for quite a long way. May be seen swimming, but also very often walking on land beside water.

Crane
Megalornis grus

Length 1·115 metres. Large bird with long legs and neck. Grey with white stripe on sides of head and neck. Red patch on head. Flies with neck outstretched. Found in marshy areas and along rivers, but also in fields. Breeds in northern Europe, but during winter flies to southern parts of Spain and Italy, and to north Africa. Rarely seen in Britain.

Moorhen
Gallinula chloropus

Length 320mm. Very common on ponds and lakes and around edges.

Black with white patch under tail and white line on sides. Red beak and 'forehead'. Very long toes but feet *not* webbed. Tail flicked when swimming and walking. Nests in bushes near water, or may make floating nest attached to plants. Name comes from 'merehen' meaning 'lake bird'.

Marsh harrier
Circus aeruginosus

Length up to 550mm. Medium-sized bird of prey with large wings and long tail. Mainly dark brown but male has grey tail and large grey wing patches. Common over much of Europe, but rarely in Britain. May be seen hunting for food over reed beds, gliding with occasional slow wing-beats.

Bittern
Botaurus stellaris

Length 760mm. Lives where there are large reed beds. Common over most of Europe south of Scandinavia, but in Britain, only in the east. Very shy. Long legs and beak. Fawn colour, mottled and streaked with darker brown and black. When alarmed, 'freezes' with neck and beak stretched upwards to blend perfectly with the reeds. Call is a booming sound.

Kingfisher
Alcedo atthis

Length 170mm. Very brightly coloured with blue and green upper parts and orange-red underneath; white throat and patch on each side of neck. Seen mostly around rivers and streams often perched on overhanging branch ready to dive for fish. Nests in hole in bank which birds make with beak. No nesting material used, but young are soon surrounded by fish bones.

Dipper
Cinclus cinclus

Length 180mm. A bird of fast mountain streams where it wades, dives, swims and walks along the bottom. Stands on rocks and bobs up and down. Dark brown with white breast. British birds have reddish-brown colour underneath. Short tail cocked slightly upwards. Nest large and domed. Quite common for it to be made behind a waterfall so parents must fly through spray to feed young.

Mammals

Otter
Lutra lutra
Body length 620–830mm, tail 365–550mm. Large mammal of rivers, lakes and canals. Long body, slim. Ears small. Long, thick tail. Short legs and webbed feet. Excellent diver and swimmer. Very playful and families may make slides down river bank. Seen mainly at night; sleeps in hollow tree or among roots. Makes whistling noise but screams and growls also. Found by lakes and streams over almost the whole of Europe.

Water shrew
Neomys fodiens
Body length 70–90mm, tail 50–70 mm. Upper parts dark grey, sometimes almost black; white or grey underneath. Tail has double row of stiff hairs underneath, making a keel. Active day and night. When swimming has a silvery appearance because of air bubbles trapped in fur. Typical shrew's long, pointed muzzle. Found close to water always, usually slow-running streams. Not found in Spain, Portugal, or Ireland.

Water vole
Arvicola terrestris
Body length 160–220mm, tail 98–144mm. Largest of the European voles. Sometimes wrongly called water rat, but has vole's typical blunter head and smaller ears. Often seen during day by pond-side, or

swimming. Makes holes in banks with entrance under water. May dig long tunnels. Found mainly in Spain, France and England. In other countries ground vole more common.

Reptiles

Grass snake
Natrix natrix
Length may be over 1 metre. Common over much of Europe. Sometimes known as ringed snake because of yellow band behind head. Body colour greyish-green, but varies. Excellent swimmer, feeding mainly on fish, frogs and newts. Other small animals also eaten. Female lays thirty to forty eggs in summer. Not venomous but may squirt evil-smelling, yellow fluid from vent if handled.

Amphibians

Marsh frog
Rana ridibunda
Length up to 170mm. Largest of the European frogs. Greyish-brown with light green on back and small, black patches. Found mainly in eastern Europe, northern part of Germany and Holland. Introduced to England. Prefers slow-moving rivers and lakes. Males very noisy in early summer.

Common frog
Rana temporaria
Length up to 80mm. Colour varies but usually shades of yellow and brown with dark brown patches and bars. Naked, smooth, moist skin. Long hind legs and webbed feet, shorter front legs. Leaps well. Jelly-like egg-masses, or spawn, laid in ponds. Eggs become tadpoles which live in water until changes have taken place in body to enable them to become land-living.

Crested newt
Triturus cristatus
Length 180mm. Looks like a lizard but is an amphibian and has no scales. Warty skin. Dark brown, covered with black spots; a white stripe on each side of tail. Underparts yellow or orange. Male has crest along back. Tail flattened from side to side and used for swimming. Prefers deep ponds with plenty of weed.

Smooth newt
Triturus vulgaris
Length 110mm. Common over much of Europe. Pale brown with darker spots. Yellow or orange underparts with black spots. In breeding season colours are brighter and male grows crest along back and tail. Breeds in ponds of almost any size, even small ones in gardens. Adults leave water after breeding and in autumn and winter may be found curled up under stones.

Fire salamander
Salamandra salamandra
Smooth, moist, naked skin. Black with bright yellow patches. Widespread in central and southern Europe but not found in Britain. Colours gave rise to the old idea that it could go through fire unharmed. Actually they are warning colours. Lives around streams and becomes active in the evening.

 Fish

Stickleback
Gasterosteus aculeatus
Length 80mm. Blue-black or green above, pale below. Three spines on back. In spring and early summer male's colours become brighter; clear green back, red throat and belly; eyes blue. Colours help to attract females to nest made of pieces of weed at bottom of stream. After eggs have been laid, male looks after them and also young when eggs have hatched.

Common bream
Abramis brama
Length 300–400mm, although occasionally up to 600mm. Very deep body, rather flattened from side to side. Dark back and golden-coloured sides. Most likely to be found in very slow-running rivers and lakes, with muddy bottoms. Feeds on pond snails, worms, etc. and holds body with head down and tail up when feeding. Commonly eaten in many European countries.

Common carp
Cyprinus carpio
Length 200mm–1 metre. Found in still or slow-running water with plenty of weed and muddy bottom. Varies in colour with bluish-green or brownish-green above, and yellowish sides. Very long-lived. Possibly introduced into Europe from Asia by the Romans and eaten as a delicacy in some countries. Much prized by anglers because of the great size it may attain. Mainly a plant-eater, but also eats some worms and insects.

Roach
Rutilis rutilis
Length up to 250mm. Found in lowland rivers and lakes throughout western Europe. Silvery fish with dark, bluish-black back. Fins on underparts of body orange-red. Lives in groups, feeding on water insects, snails and leeches as well as seeds and some weeds. Lays its eggs in spring among weeds at water's edge. Very similar in appearance to rudd which lives in same kind of places.

Perch
Perca fluviatilis
Length up to 250mm. Found in rivers and lakes over most of Europe, except for far north and south. Back and

sides green with several black bands running from back down sides. Lower fins red. Large fin on back with strong, sharp spines. Lives in groups. Eats smaller fish. Eggs are laid in sticky, lace-like bands which float and then become attached to water plants.

Eel
Anguilla anguilla
Length up to 1 metre. Long, narrow, snake-like body; greenish-brown above and silvery below. Lives in rivers and lakes until ready to breed, then swims to sea and across the Atlantic to Sargasso Sea. After mating, adult eels die and young find their way back to Europe, taking up to three years for the journey. When first hatched, young eel is flattened and only gradually gains typical eel shape.

Pike
Esox lucius
Length 250mm—1·5 metres. Found in rivers and lakes throughout Europe. Long, pointed head and long body with black fin close to tail. Greeny-brown, sides with golden patches, but colours vary. Lies in wait among plants and attacks other creatures for food. Young pike eat insect larvae and young fish. Older ones will catch larger fish and even water birds such as moorhens.

Salmon
Salmo salar
Large fish, greenish or brown mottled with orange and dark spots when in fresh-water, but greener and more silvery in sea. In breeding season adults struggle up rivers to fast-running upper parts where bottom is gravel. There they spawn and usually die. Young live in river but after a few years swim to sea and live there, but return to same river to breed. A very valuable food fish.

 Invertebrates

Water scorpion
Nepa cinerea
Not related to land scorpion but is a water bug up to 20mm long, found in weedy ponds over much of Europe. Very well-camouflaged with muddy-coloured, leaf-shaped body, flat and with a long, thin breathing-tube at the hind end. Two front legs are thickened and are used to hold prey which is caught by darting out from among weeds.

Dragonfly
Anax imperator
Length about 75mm. Long, slender-bodied insect with very large eyes. Two pairs of transparent wings with network of veins over them. Wing-span about 105mm. Colour of body blue and black in male, but female is greener. Other species of dragon-flies may be blue and brown, yellow and black, or all red or green. Flies quickly and darts about catching other insects, or may hover. Eggs are laid in water and hatch into nymphs.

Dragonfly larva
Dragonfly larvae, or nymphs, live in weedy ponds and slow-running streams. They are rather sluggish and body is 20—30mm long; rather plump and muddy-coloured. They catch other pond creatures by means of the 'mask' which is a pair of pincers that can be shot forward from under the head. After a long period of living under water, the nymphs climb up a plant stem into the air. Skin splits and adults emerge.

Damselfly
Agrion splendens
Length 47mm. Long, very slender body. Red eyes. Two pairs of gauzy wings with network of veins and large dark blue blotch on each wing. Damselflies are similar in appearance

to dragonflies but have much slimmer bodies and are usually smaller. They rest with their wings held together over their body, whereas dragonflies rest with theirs out sideways.

Damselfly larva

Delicate animal that crawls among plants and on bottom of ponds. Slender body with three, large, leaf-like gills at end. Wing buds can be seen on back. Three pairs of legs. Head with large eyes and 'mask' for catching prey underneath, as with dragonly larva. Dull colour for camouflage. Body length 26mm plus 12mm for gills. Some species are smaller.

Mayfly

Species of *Ephemera*

Delicate insect with slim body and three long 'tails'. Dull yellow except for front part of body which is black. Wings glisten and show network of veins. Front wings longer than hind wings. Delicate legs. Many species of mayflies, some with only two 'tails'. Rests with wings folded upright over body. Emerges from water-living nymph and lives just long enough to mate and lay eggs, which may be as little as one day.

Mayfly larva

Slender, very delicate creature that buries itself in tunnel in bank of stream or lake. Body with three, long 'tails' at end and seven pairs of small, feathery gills along sides. Length 15–23mm. Some species live in fast-running streams and have flattened bodies so they will not be swept away as they cling to stones. These species have extremely long 'tails'.

Caddisfly

Many species, very similar and not easy to identify. Medium-sized insect, usually found near water. Dull-coloured, brown or greyish, and resembles moth. Two pairs of wings

covered with tiny hairs, held over back when at rest making roof-shape. Usually flies at dusk. Very long, thin antennae on head, often longer than wings. Length about 20mm with closed wings.

Caddisfly larva

Many different species. Found in rivers, ponds and streams. Body slim and soft. Makes protective tube from sand and grains, small shells, leaf fragments or pieces of twig. Material used depends on species and cases vary from 10–30mm long. Most larvae are plant feeders but a few eat small water animals.

Pondskater

Gerris lacustris

Very common small insect found on still water all over Europe. Body about 15mm long, with much longer legs. Middle pair 'row' the insect across the surface and the back pair act as a rudder. The shorter front legs are used for catching small insects which have fallen on water and on which it feeds.

Whirligig beetle

Gyrinus natator

Small water beetle, about 5mm long. Spends most of its time whirling round and round on the surface of still or slow-moving water in ponds and ditches. When disturbed it dives. Shining black body. Back legs flattened and covered with hairs. Eyes divided into two parts; upper part used for seeing in air and lower part used under water. Often seen in large numbers in summer, but go into mud for winter.

Water spider

Argyroneta aquatica

Typical spider shape, up to 15mm long. Brown, but may look silvery under water because of air trapped against body. Collects bubbles of air at surface, takes them down and releases them under a web which it spins between stems of water plant. The webb becomes bell-shaped and spider lives in this, leaving it to catch small water creatures which are brought back to be eaten.

Water boatmen
Notonecta glauca
Length about 20mm. Found in most ponds. Body brownish-black and boat-shaped. Swims on back, 'rowing' itself along with long hind legs which are fringed with hairs. Keeps coming to surface to renew air-bubble which it must carry for breathing. Feeds on any living creature it can find, even quite large fish. Painful bite if handled carelessly.

Great diving beetle
Dytiscus marginalis
Large beetle, up to 30mm long, found in weedy ponds and lakes throughout Britain and north and central Europe. Good swimmer. Black or brownish-black with dull yellow border. Breathes air and carries supply under wing-cases. Attacks fish, newts and water insects. Can give a painful bite. Larva also lives in ponds and is even more ferocious than adult.

Swan mussel
Anodonta cygnaea
Hinged shell, more or less oval shape, up to 250mm long but may be as little as 95mm. Colour varies but is usually yellowish-green or brown. Lives in muddy, slow-moving rivers or canals, where it lies half-buried in mud. Feeds by filtering particles from water.

Great pond snail
Limnaea stagnalis
Large snail of lowland ponds. Thin shell up to 60mm high. Circular breathing hole behind head. Feeds mainly on plants but will also eat dead beetle larvae or small fish. Rasps away at food with a rough tongue, or *radula*, which has rows and rows of fine teeth across it. If pond dries up, snail withdraws into shell and forms a tough layer across opening so that body remains moist.

Ramshorn snail
Planorbis corneus
Flat spiral shell with glossy surface that has fine lines around it. Animal itself is dark brown or red. Found in slow-moving water or still pond where there is plenty of weed. Can survive dry periods in same way as great pond snail. There are many species of ramshorn snails; *Planorbis corneus* is the largest and has a shell 30mm across.

Crayfish
Potamobius astacus
Length up to 200mm. Looks like a small lobster. Flattened tail, eight walking legs and two claws for holding food. Underside of pincers reddish and so crayfish sometimes called red-claw. Feeds mainly on animals such as water-snails, insect larvae, worms, etc. In Britain a smaller crayfish, *Potamobius pallipes*, is native species. Length about 100mm. Greenish-brown. Found in streams in limestone country. Not as common as it was.

Trees & Shrubs

Alder
Ht up to 20m
(p85)

Goat willow
Ht 3 – 10m
(p85)

White willow
Ht 10 – 20m
(p85)

Herbs

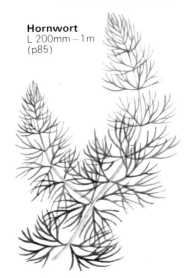

Hornwort
L 200mm – 1m
(p85)

Duckweed
'Leaves' 4mm across
(p85)

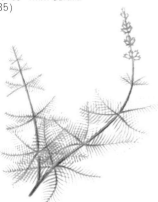

Water milfoil
L 0.5 – 2.5m
(p85)

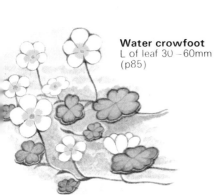

Water crowfoot
L of leaf 30 – 60mm
(p85)

Water-lily
200mm across
(p86)

Arrowhead
L of leaf 50–200mm
(p86)

Common reed
Ht up to 3m
(p86)

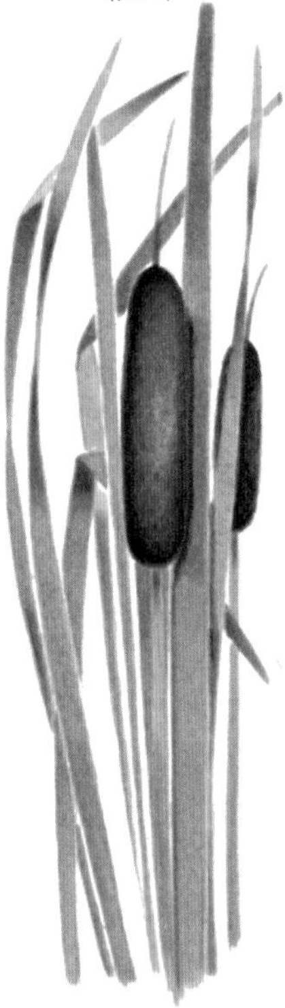

Reedmace
Ht up to 3m
(p86)

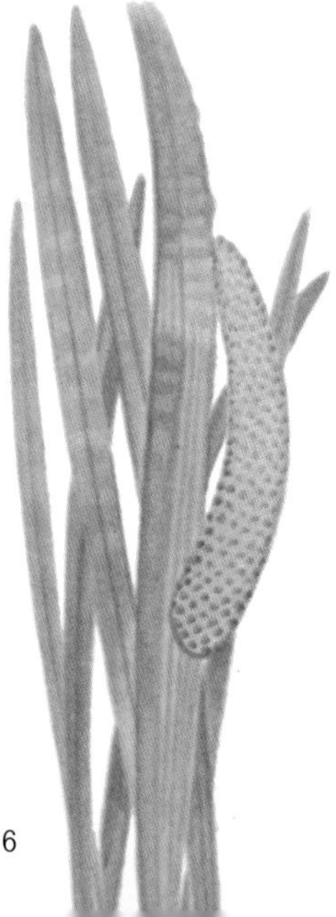

Sweet flag
Ht up to 1m
(p86)

Bur-reed
Ht up to 1·25m
(p86)

Iris
0.5 – 1.5m
(p86)

Purple loosestrife
Ht 600mm – 1.2m
(p87)

Water forget-me-not
L 150 – 450mm
(p87)

Great willow-herb
Ht up to 1.5m
(p86)

Meadowsweet
Ht 600mm – 1.2m
(p87)

97

Birds

Mallard
L 590mm
(p87)

Grey heron
L 1m
(p87)

Great crested grebe
L 450mm
(p87)

Mute swan
L 1·5m
(p87)

Dabchick
L 250mm
(p88)

Coot
L 370mm
(p88)

Crane
L 1·115m
(p88)

Marsh harrier
L up to 550mm
(p88)

Moorhen
L 320mm
(p88)

Kingfisher
L 170mm
(p88)

Dipper
L 180mm
(p88)

Bittern
L 760mm
(p88)

Mammals

Otter
BL 620 – 830mm
(p89)

Water shrew
BL 70 – 90mm
(p89)

Water vole
BL 160 – 220mm
(p89)

Reptiles

Amphibians

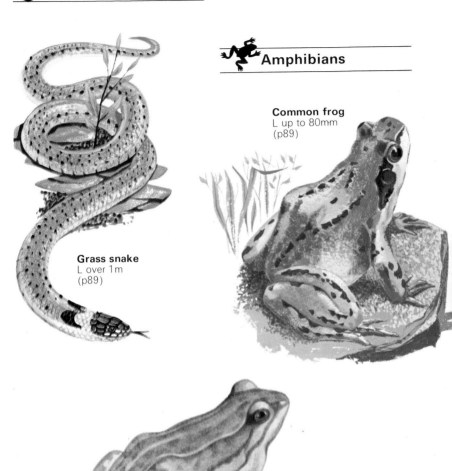

Common frog
L up to 80mm
(p89)

Grass snake
L over 1m
(p89)

Marsh frog
L up to 170mm
(p89)

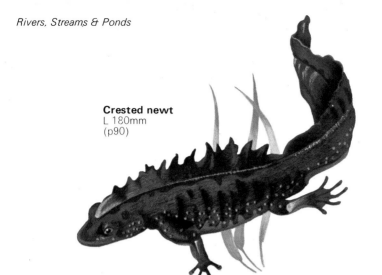

Crested newt
L 180mm
(p90)

Fire salamander
L 130 – 162mm
(p90)

Smooth newt
L 110mm
(p90)

Fish

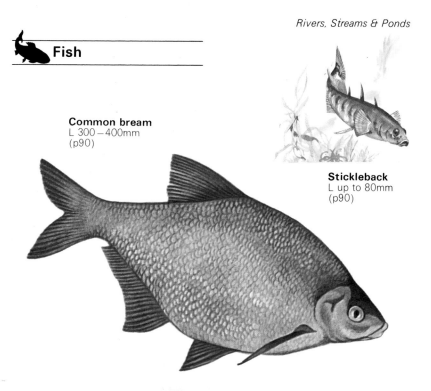

Common bream
L 300 – 400mm
(p90)

Stickleback
L up to 80mm
(p90)

Common carp
L 200mm – 1m
(p90)

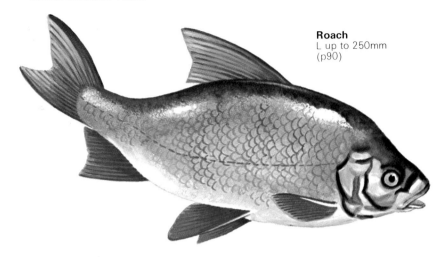

Roach
L up to 250mm
(p90)

Perch
L up to 250mm
(p90)

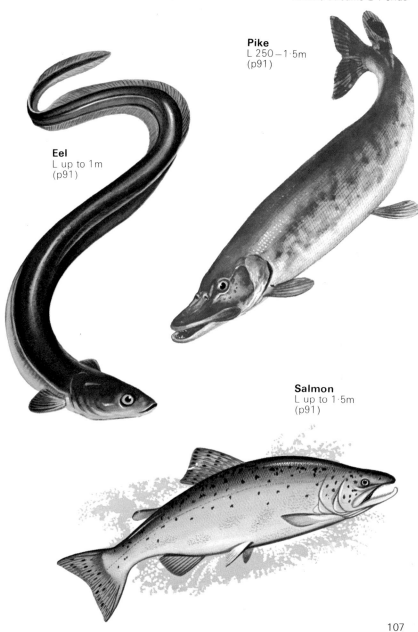

Pike
L 250 – 1·5m
(p91)

Eel
L up to 1m
(p91)

Salmon
L up to 1·5m
(p91)

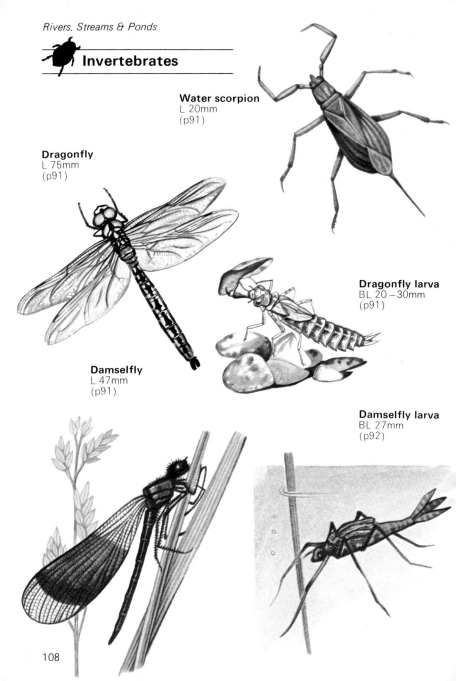

Invertebrates

Water scorpion
L 20mm
(p91)

Dragonfly
L 75mm
(p91)

Dragonfly larva
BL 20–30mm
(p91)

Damselfly
L 47mm
(p91)

Damselfly larva
BL 27mm
(p92)

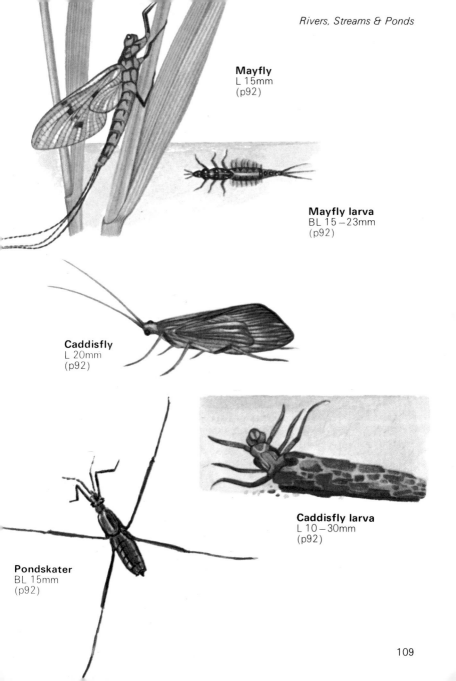

Mayfly
L 15mm
(p92)

Mayfly larva
BL 15–23mm
(p92)

Caddisfly
L 20mm
(p92)

Caddisfly larva
L 10–30mm
(p92)

Pondskater
BL 15mm
(p92)

Water boatman
L 20mm
(p93)

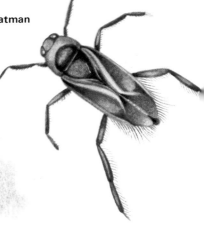

Whirligig beetle
L 5mm
(p92)

Great diving beetle
L up to 30mm
(p93)

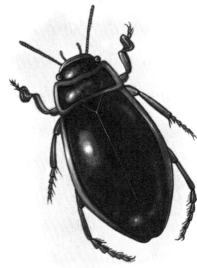

Water spider
L up to 15mm
(p92)

Swan mussel
L of shell 95—250mm
(p93)

Great pond snail
Ht of shell 60mm
(p93)

Crayfish
L up to 200mm
(p93)

Ramshorn snail
Shell 30mm across
(p93)

Seashores

Wherever land and sea meet there is some type of seashore and there are many thousands of kilometres of shore around the coast of Europe.

Some shores are rocky and others covered with shingle, while some are mainly of sand or mud. The type of shore depends on whether the rocks that make the land at that point are hard or soft and whether the waves are likely to break up those rocks. It also depends on whether the sea there is depositing sand and moving pebbles, or taking them away to deposit somewhere else. It may also depend on whether a river happens to run into the sea just there.

Very few shores belong only to one type. Rocks, pebbles and sand may all be found within a few metres of each other, or perhaps sand will merge into mud further along the beach.

Rocky shores are always very attractive and it is here that rock pools may be found. The best shores for finding sea creatures and plants are where the rocks are very hard; although it may take a long time for pieces of the cliff to break off and fall, when they do they will not be worn too smooth by the waves. As a result there will be plenty of places where small plants and animals can cling.

Shingle beaches are made up of pebbles which are always being rolled as the waves rush over them. Nothing much can live on a shingle beach like that, but it can be a wonderful place if you are a pebble collector.

Sandy shores are made of small particles of very hard minerals, often the glassy-looking fragments of silica.

There are plenty of animals that live on sandy shores, but they cannot afford to be exposed as they might be eaten, or else dry up. Often digging is the only way to find the inhabitants of the sandy shore.

Muddy shores are found where the land is made of clay, but also in estuaries where rivers widen and river and sea waters mix. Mud is made up of very fine particles, some from rock and others of plant and animal remains. The mud usually builds up to form *mud flats* which have very little slope, but provide plenty of food for certain animals.

About every 12·5 hours, a shore is covered and uncovered again by the tide. But each tide does not cover the same amount of the shore. Some reach high up on the shore and go out a long way. These very high and very low tides are the *spring tides*, although despite their name, they occur not only in the spring, but every month. At other times the water does not come up so high nor go out so far. This happens at the time of the *neap tides*.

It is useful when studying the shore to think of it as being divided up into a number of *zones*. The

Lots of tiny animals lie buried underneath the sand.

Rock pools contain creatures that cannot survive long out of the sea.

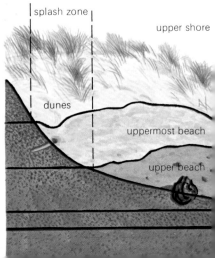

highest part above the high tide mark which is only splashed by spray is the *splash zone*. That part of the shore that is covered only by the high spring tides is the *upper shore*. The *middle shore* is the part most often covered by the average high tides and uncovered as far as the level of average low tides, while the *lower shore* is only uncovered at low spring tides. Lower than that is the *sub-littoral zone* which always has shallow water over it.

114

Life on Seashores

To the holiday-maker, the seashore is a delightful place, but to the animals and plants that live there it is a place of enormous problems. Because the tides cover and uncover the shore twice a day, those plants and animals must be adapted for living in water, and yet must still be able to cope with the problem of drying out when they are uncovered again. How do these species manage?

Most of the seaweeds are coated with a thin layer of slime so that they will keep moist for quite a long time. It is this slime that makes seaweed-covered rocks so slippery to walk upon. A few seaweeds that are found on the upper shore are able to remain out of the water for days on end, especially at the time of the neap tides. They become black, very dry and shrivelled, but as soon as

The shore zones related to tide levels. Many plants and animals are only found in one particular zone and so it is convenient to use these terms to describe whereabouts on the shore you should look for certain seaweeds or animals.

the tide reaches them once more, they absorb water rapidly to regain their proper shape and colour.

Seaweed provides food for many animals, and shelter also. It is the perfect hiding place when the tide is out. Beneath the weed it is cool, moist and out of sight of birds which are looking for a meal. Lift up a piece and under it you are likely to find more than one species of periwinkle, small shore crabs and large numbers of sand hoppers.

On a rocky shore, there will be animals clinging to the cool, shady sides of the rocks. Sea anemones look like blobs of jelly, their tentacles pulled in for the time being. Sea slaters and small molluscs will have found the cracks and squeezed into them. Some of the larger molluscs, limpets for example, will have pulled their shells down hard against the rock, trapping a little water under them as they do so. Where there are rock pools, the animals trapped in them when the tide goes out will have fewer problems than those left exposed. At least they will have water, even if space is limited.

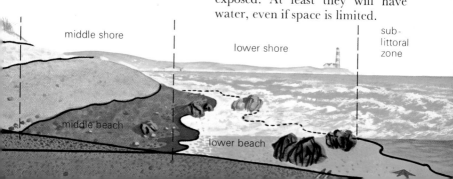

middle shore

lower shore

sub-littoral zone

middle beach

lower beach

Those animals that live on sandy and muddy shores are often the burrowers. Lugworms and razor shells are very different kinds of animals, yet they both solve their problems by burrowing, staying safely beneath the sand and mud while the tide is out. They often burrow while the tide is in too, for they are able to feed while they remain there covered by the water and surrounded by muddy sand.

Once the tide returns, all the animals can begin to feed again. The shore crabs, which are scavengers, crowd in towards any dead creature on the sea bed, tearing pieces from it with their claws. In fact, a good way to catch crabs is to tie a piece of string to a bone left over from a joint of meat that you may have had for a meal; just leave it in the sea for ten minutes or so. When it is gently pulled out again, it will be covered with crabs clinging to it, attracted by the meat still left on the bone, and feeding on it.

Some animals, though, are filterers, taking in water and straining food particles from it before returning the water to the sea again. Most of the molluscs with hinged shells, the *bivalves*, such as cockles and mussels, feed in this way. Their bodies are buried in the sand but two tubes, or *siphons*, reach up to the water which is sucked in through

The common mussel is a bivalve. It attaches itself to rocks and piers by means of long threads and feeds by straining water through its syphon and gills.

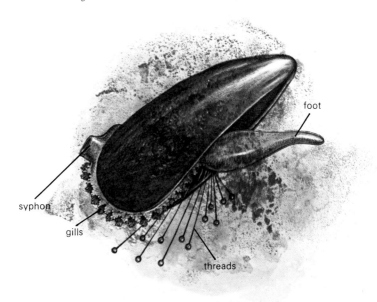

foot

syphon

gills

threads

syphon

operculum

tentacles

foot

The common whelk is a gastropod. The *operculum* (a horny substance) acts like a door, plugging the shell's aperture when the animal withdraws into it.

one and blown out again through the other.

The snail-like molluscs, or *gastropods*, such as whelks, have rasping tongues covered with rows of tiny, spiked teeth. Some gastropods scrape off small plants from the rocks, but others can make holes in the shells of other molluscs and eat the soft body inside.

Sea anemones have stinging cells in their tentacles which can stun or kill small fish and shrimps that happen to touch them. The dead animal is then pulled into the anemone's mouth which lies in the middle of the tentacles.

Where shores are rocky, it is very obvious that the plants and animals there do not live just anywhere, but in the various areas or zones mentioned in the introduction to this chapter. Which particular zone they live in depends on how well they are adapted to shore life. This zonation is easiest to see in the brown seaweeds. High up on the shore grows the small channelled wrack, which can withstand being dried for long periods. Just a little lower down may be the spiral wrack which can also be left uncovered for a long time without damage. (Spiral wrack gets its name from the way that the fronds often have a twist in them.)

On the middle shore where the seaweeds will not be out of the water for any great length of time the knotted wrack with its narrow fronds and very large air-bladders will be found. Nearer low tide mark this will be replaced by the toothed wrack, so called because of the jagged edges to its fronds, and the bladder wrack, with pairs of small air-bladders that help it to float upright in the water.

Those parts of the shore that are only uncovered when the spring tides go out a long way are where the large oar weeds are to be found.

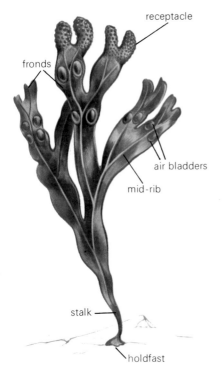

receptacle

fronds

air bladders

mid-rib

stalk

holdfast

The structure of a common seaweed.

Once the idea of zonation is understood, then much more can be done investigating zonation in animals, especially those such as periwinkles, limpets and barnacles. Sandy shores have their zonations too. The inhabitants of the shore will vary according to the part of Europe they are in. Those of Scandinavia will not be the same as those of the west coast of England, for example, so there is plenty to interest the keen naturalist everywhere.

Birds are plentiful around the coast, and like all animals, they are adapted to a particular way of life. There are birds such as the puffins and gannets that are really birds of the sea and spend most of their time fishing far away from land, but they must return to the rocky cliffs to breed.

Others are wading birds, preferring to paddle along the water's edge and probe into the sand and mud for food. Curlew and dunlin are examples of waders. Ducks and geese, although not waders, can be seen in estuaries and by muddy shores, some eating weed and others feeding on the small worms and molluscs they find there.

Rocky shores are good places to look for fossils although you will not find them in all types of rock. Fossils are the remains or traces of animals and plants that lived millions of years ago. The bones or shells of many of the animals have been preserved in the rocks which were once part of the sea bed, and have themselves been turned into stone. Common ones which may be found are belemnites, which look like bullets, and ammonites. These are coiled shells that belonged to squid-like animals whose soft bodies were protected inside these shells.

There may be shells very similar to modern ones and possibly even bones or teeth of prehistoric reptiles and mammals. The type of fossil you may find will depend upon the age of the rocks you are looking at.

Things to look for on Seashores

 ## Herbs

Marram grass
Ammophila arenaria
A tough grass, 600mm–1·20 metres high, which grows on sand dunes. Spreads by means of underground stems which send down roots and help to bind sand together. Leaves rolled to cut down water loss. Flowers form whitish spike at the end of stalk. Sometimes deliberately planted to stop spread of loose sand.

Glasswort
Salicornia europea
A low growing, very fleshy plant of muddy salt-marshes. Stems branching. Leaves like scales. Whole plant dark green, which may become yellowish and then reddish. Plants very numerous on bare mud, often covering several hectares. Once gathered and burnt so that ash could be used in glassmaking. Young stems may be pickled and eaten. Also called marsh samphire.

Thrift
Armeria maritima
Low growing plant, found growing on cliffs and also covering large areas of salt-marsh. Leaves very narrow, 20–150mm long, plentiful and closely packed so that whole plant forms a cushion. Flowers small, pink and grouped in ball-shaped clusters at top of stem 50–120mm high.

Sea holly
Eryngium maritimum
Sea holly is found mainly among sand dunes, but also on some shingle beaches. Height 300–600mm. Branching. Blue-grey colour. Leaves very waxy and spiny, veins and edges white. Flowers blue, in thistle-like clusters at end of stem, with spiny bracts, like leaves, underneath flower-mass. Roots were once gathered and candied to be eaten as sweets. In some parts of England it was all dug up for this and can no longer be found.

Sea lavender
Limonium vulgare
Common plant of salt-marshes. Leaves more or less oval, becoming narrower towards stem, growing close to the ground as a rosette. Flowers bluish-purple, in clusters on stems 80–300mm high which branch near the top. Often picked and dried for decoration. Not related to garden lavender and gets its name only from the colour of the flowers which is similar.

 ## Seaweeds

Toothed wrack
Fucus serratus
Brown seaweed found covering rocks on lower middle shore. Fronds about 600mm long, flattened, with a thick midrib. Easily recognised by edges of fronds which are toothed like a saw. May be possible to see clusters of very tiny hairs along fronds. Pin-head size bumps which may be seen at the ends of seaweed are reproductive parts of seaweed. Very common and often found in very large amounts.

Carragheen
Chondrus crispus
Dark red seaweed with flat fronds branching in a regular way. Up to 150mm long. Sometimes has a stalk but may not if growing in sheltered place. Attached to rocks by small

disc. Varies a great deal in shape. Common on middle shore and likely to be found in rock pools. Eaten in Ireland and sometimes called Irish moss.

Bladderwort
Fucus vesiculosus
Very common and plentiful brown seaweed of the middle shore. Fronds 150mm–1 metre long with smooth edges that may be torn. Very distinct midrib. Easily identified by air-bladders, usually in pairs on either side of midrib. Tips of some fronds may be yellowish, swollen and covered with tiny bumps. These are reproductive parts.

Oar weed
Laminaria saccharina
This oar weed is also called sea belt. Very large, brown seaweed with frond 200mm–3 metres long. Stalk has holdfast on the end that looks like a tangle of roots. Frond ribbon-like but crinkled. Several species of oar weeds, all of them large and many having a very wide frond divided into a number of strap-like pieces. All of them are usually only uncovered during spring tides, but they are sometimes washed up after storms.

Sea lettuce
Ulva lactuca
Green seaweed which is pale green when young and darker green when old. Forms flattened sheets up to 400–500mm long, but usually much smaller. May have a short, solid stalk. Common on rocky shores and in rock pools especially where there is some fresh water, for example where a stream trickles down.

Corallina
Corallina officinalis
Red seaweed, common in rock pools of the middle shore. Grows in tufts, 50–120mm high, attached to rocks. Stems and branches have a hard, lime coat which makes the plant look a little like coral. Branches and branchlets opposite one another. Colour varies from dark red to almost white.

Birds

Great black-backed gull
Larus marinus
Length 680mm. Very large gull. Recognised by black back, pink legs, and large size. Will feed on almost any kind of animal food such as dead fish, and will also raid colonies of seabirds for eggs and young. Lesser black-backed gull is similar in colour but legs are yellow. In Britain the back of lesser black-backed may be grey rather than black. Length 520mm. Found around coast, but inland also, unlike great black-backed which rarely comes inland.

Common tern
Sterna hirundo
Length 350mm. Slim bird with very pointed wings and long, forked tail. Most of body is white, but top of head and back of neck are black. Beak long, pointed and red with black tip. Legs red. Graceful flier, now and again diving straight into water for fish. Often in groups when they may be noisy, screaming after one that has caught a fish.

Herring gull
Larus argentatus
Length 560mm. Large gull. Mainly white, but grey back and black tips to wings. Yellow beak with red spot. Pink legs, but those in Mediterranean region may have yellow legs. Common all over Europe, not only along seashore but also by rivers and lakes, and on rubbish dumps. Used to nest only on cliffs but will now nest on buildings near coast and inland by lakes.

Puffin
Fratercula arctica
Length 300mm. Stout body and large head. Black back and top of head, white underparts and face. Large beak which is brightly coloured in breeding season, rather less so at other times. A bird of open sea most of the year, but coming to the coast of north-west Europe to nest in burrows during the summer. Burrows are usually on cliff tops and may be old rabbit burrows, or may be dug by birds themselves.

Razorbill
Alca torda
Length 400mm. White underparts and rest of bird black except for narrow white stripe on wings and white line on sides of face. Heavy beak. Tends to stand rather upright. Spends much of the time well out to sea, but breeds on cliffs and rocky shores. Lays single egg in hollow on cliff or under rock on shore without any nesting material. Egg very pointed to prevent rolling away when left.

Gannet
Sula bassana
Length 900mm. White body, black wing-tips, golden yellow head with black markings around eyes. Pale blue beak. Very long, narrow wings best seen in flight. Winters spent out at sea, coming to a few rocky shores only to breed in spring. Catches fish by diving from height of 15 metres or more, or by swimming under water.

Cormorant
Phalacrocorax carbo
Length 950mm. Black feathers with greenish gloss on them. Long, hooked beak. White chin. White patch on thighs in summer. Stands fairly upright when resting and may have wings outstretched to dry. Common around coasts but also along large rivers and around lakes. Eats large numbers of fish every day. Nests mostly on cliffs but occasionally in trees inland.

Guillemot
Uria aalge
Length 400mm. Very much like razorbill in general shape and appearance but has slimmer and more pointed beak. The neck is thinner and back as well as back of head are dark brown rather than black, although this is difficult to see from a distance. Winter spent at sea. Breeds around coasts of north-west Europe and Portugal laying single egg on cliff ledge without making nest.

Avocet
Recurvirostra avosetta
Length 425mm. Seen in sheltered bays and estuaries in some parts of Holland, Denmark, France, Spain and parts of England. Striking black and white pattern, long legs, slim neck and head, long, graceful, upturned beak. The black and white pattern very clearly seen in flight. In Holland it is called *kluut*, which is the call the bird makes.

Flamingo
Phoenicopterus ruber
Length 1·25 metres. Large bird not likely to be mistaken for any other. Very long legs and neck; strange shaped beak, stout with end half sharply down-curved. Body pink with brighter red legs. Wings bright pink and black, pattern showing when in flight. Likely to be seen only in the Carmargue in southern France, and in southern Spain. Young flamingoes are grey and do not get their adult colour until they are about eighteen months old.

Spoonbill
Platalea leucorodia
Length 860mm. Related to herons and storks. Large white bird with

long legs and unusual spoon-shaped beak. Large wings, best seen when in flight. Flies with neck outstretched. Found in southern Spain and eastern Europe, where there is shallow water, and in marshes and lagoons. Nests in reeds or in trees.

Oystercatcher
Haematopus ostralegus
Length 430mm. Black and white; long red beak and red legs. Common around all coasts, wading along the edge of the water probing for molluscs. Despite its name, it rarely eats oysters. Usually in groups. In flight the wide white wing stripes and white rump show up clearly. Very shrill, piping call when alarmed.

Curlew
Numenius arquata
Length 550mm. Fairly large wading bird with long downward-curved beak. Dull brown with darker brown stripes and spots. In winter, can be seen on mud-flats probing in mud for worms and small molluscs. Breeding takes place away from coast, often on moorland where nest is made among heather. Cry is 'cur-lew' which has given rise to its name.

Dunlin
Calidris alpina
Length 180mm. Common small wading bird with short legs and rather long beak. Winter colouring is greyish-brown above and white below. In summer, back is rusty brown and belly is black. Often seen in large flocks, possibly with other species of waders. Nests on moors and marshes. Also known by many other names, including ox-bird, sea-snipe and stint.

Shelduck
Tadorna tadorna
Length 650mm. Large duck, common around muddy parts of the coast and estuaries, and on some lakes inland.

Bold pattern of white, brown and black. Red beak; the drake has a red knob at the base. Nests in rabbit burrows or under bushes on shore.

Scoter
Melanitta nigra
Length 480mm. Drake is all black with orange patch on beak. Duck is dark brown with lighter cheeks. Breeds in Scandinavia, making nest in hollows on ground along shores of lakes or rivers. Between April and September may be seen around coasts of western Europe on sea close to shore.

Eider
Somateria mollissima
Length 600mm. Drake white above and black below. Duck brown mottled with black. No angle between top of beak and forehead; they join in almost straight line. Nests along shores of north-west Europe and female plucks down from her breast to line nest. In some places this is collected and used as filling for pillows and eiderdowns. Outside breeding season, eiders are usually at sea.

 # Fish

Lumpsucker
Cyclopterus lumpus
Really a shore fish, but small ones sometimes stranded in rock pools. Deep, rounded body with rows of hard bumps along back and sides. Usually about 150mm long. Male is reddish colour but females are dark blue. The sucker from which fish gets its name is underneath body. Fish uses it for holding onto rocks.

Cuckoo wrasse
Labrus mixtus
Length up to 350mm. Quite heavily built fish with thick lips and strong

teeth. Long fin on back. Male has blue head and sides, and blue patches on fins and tail. Rest of body orange. Female is mainly orange and has three dark patches on back towards tail. Several species of wrasse and most are colourful. Mainly shore fish but small ones are sometimes found in rock pools.

Goby
Gobius minutus
Often seen in rock pools although really a shore fish. Length 60–90mm. Colour varies, but usually grey above and four dark bands down sides. Two fins on back and first one nearest head has dark blue spot on it in the male. Swims in shoals and is common in estuaries or where it is sandy and the water shallow.

Lesser weever
Trachinus vipera
Length up to 150mm. Common in shallow waters around coasts and sandy bays of Europe during summer. Lies buried in sand, looking for food. Greyish-fawn above, lighter below. Faint darker lines along sides. Large mouth and eyes near top of head. Two fins on back, smaller one near head is black and has about six spines. Spines on gill covers and on fins of back are venomous and cause very painful swellings. If stung by weever seek medical treatment.

Blenny
Blennius ocellaris
Length 80–170mm. Short, blunt head. Body grey with several paler stripes on sides running from back downwards. Fin on back long, but front half taller than rear and has large black spot on it, with a white edge. Two short pieces of skin stand up from head near eyes. Several kinds of blenny. The species illustrated usually called butterfly blenny (*see page 136*).

Invertebrates

Limpet
Patella vulgata
Sea snail common on rocky shores. Shell is a low cone, up to 50mm across, with ridges down it, greyish-white, thick and strong. Several species of limpets, most of them with brown or black on the outside of the shells. Limpets pull themselves down tightly onto rocks when tide is out. When covered by water they move slowly over rocks feeding on small plants growing there.

Dog whelk
Nucella lapillus
Sea snail with thick, coiled shell, up to 40mm high. Coils may be marked with ridges. Colour of shell may be white, brown, or white and brown bands. Living animal feeds on barnacles or mussels which it attacks by boring through shell with rasping tongue. Type of mollusc eaten affects colour of shell. Common on rocky shores that are not too exposed, in middle shore zone.

Mussel
Mytilus edulis
Bivalve mollusc (shell in two parts hinged together). Roughly oval shape, 10–100mm long, but one end more pointed than the other. Attached to rocks, piers, etc. in large numbers, and also muddy shores if there are stones. Attaches itself by threads which it makes. Dark blue, almost black. Filter-feeder. Often collected, cooked and eaten. Found on middle shore and downwards.

Periwinkle
Littorina littorea
Very common sea snail, found under seaweed and on rocks on middle and lower shore. Shell usually dark grey or brown, coiled, pointed, with ridges around it, 10–20mm high. Collected,

cooked and eaten. Other kinds of periwinkles are smaller and may be red, brown, orange, green or black. Commonest is the flat periwinkle, *Littorina littoralis.*

Common whelk
Buccinum undatum
Large sea snail with pointed, coiled shell, up to 80mm high, although those further away from the shore grow larger. Six or seven coils with lines and ridges on them. Usually a brown, velvety coating covers the white shell. Whelks are flesh-eating and live in the lower parts of the shore where there is muddy sand or gravel. Empty egg-cases like clumps of papery bubbles often washed up on beach.

Scallop
Pecten maximus
Shell in two parts, hinged together, one flatter than the other. Fan-shaped, with large ridges spreading out from point. On either side of point are small parts of shell spreading sideways like wings. Reddish-brown or yellowish; about 150mm across. Not usually found alive close to shore, but parts of shell often washed up. Other species of scallop are smaller and more colourful.

Razor shell
Ensis arcuatus
Shell in two parts, hinged together when alive; commonly separated when dead. Very long, up to 150mm, but not very wide. Slightly curved. Similar shape to blade of old-fashioned razor. White but covered with thin yellowish-brown layer that peels off. Lives around sandy shores. Pod razor shell is longer and straight.

Common cockle
Cardium edule
Shell in two parts, hinged together when alive; then almost ball-shaped with many ridges. Edge of shell

crinkled. About 30mm across. Brown. Found on lower shore where there is muddy sand that the animal can burrow into. May be present in huge numbers, forming cockle beds. Often collected, cooked and eaten.

Tellin
Tellina fabula
Shell in two parts, hinged together. Each part flattened for easy movement through sand. Roughly oval, 20mm long, orange or yellowish. Found at low water level in clean sand. Many species of tellins often with shell rounder in outline. Usually quite brightly coloured. Always flattened.

Sand gaper
Mya arenaria
Shell in two parts hinged together. Large, up to 120mm long, oval, grey or brownish in colour. Buries itself in sand or sandy mud, and may be found around the lower shore and downwards, but also in estuaries. Occasionally washed up in large numbers on shell banks, such as those on parts of the east coast of England.

Goose barnacle
Lepas anatifera
Does not usually live between tide-marks, but sometimes cast up. Several may be attached to a piece of driftwood. Plates white with a bluish look about them. Fleshy, blue-grey stalk. In the water, plates part to allow the six pairs of feathery limbs to comb food particles from sea. Shell about 50mm long and stalk may be up to 200mm, but often drawn up.

Acorn barnacle
Balanus balanoides
In large numbers on surface of rocks, etc., between tide marks. Looks like small, white, tent-shaped shell up to 10mm across. Made up of several side plates fixed together. Hole at top covered by smaller ones. When

covered by water, top plates open up and food is gathered from water by feathery legs. Not a mollusc, despite its appearance, but a relative of crabs and shrimps.

Sea slater
Ligia oceanica
Length up to 25mm. Body flattened, oval, with jointed shell. Seven pairs of walking legs. Two pairs of 'tails' at rear. Greyish-green colour. Related to garden woodlice and very similar shape. Found in cracks and under rocks and seaweed, high up on shore. Moves about at night to feed. Large numbers eaten by gulls and crabs.

Common shrimp
Crangon vulgaris
Body 20–60mm long, slightly flattened on top. Grey or brown, with darker spots. First pair of legs with small pincers for picking up food and second pair with even smaller pincers. Walking legs at front end of body and swimming legs towards hind end. Found in sandy places where water is shallow. Often caught in large numbers, cooked and eaten.

Sandhopper
Orchestia gammarella
Small relative of shrimps and lobsters, found in large numbers under seaweed and stones at top of beach. Body up to 20mm long, jointed skin, flattened from side to side and slightly curved. Jumps when uncovered. Wriggles on its side through sand. Feeds on rotting seaweed and animal matter.

Squat lobster
Galathea squamifera
Sometimes found under stones in rock pools of lower shore. Like small, greenish-brown lobster, up to 450mm long, with tail flap tucked under body. First pair of legs longer than body and with pincers on the end. Next three pairs of legs quite long,

but last pair small and often not noticed. Can swim backwards if startled by using tail flap. Other species of squat lobsters are orange or red.

Hermit crab
Eupagurus bernhardus
Up to 120mm long, but those usually found on the shore are more likely to be 30–80mm. Front of body and legs have hard shell, but hind part soft and twisted into empty shell, commonly whelk, for protection. One pincer larger than the other and this will block entrance to shell when crab withdraws into it. Dull red colour with some parts creamy yellow. Shell may have anemone attached to it. Common on lower shore.

Shore crab
Carcinus maenas
Crab most likely to be seen on any kind of shore. Green or greenish-brown. First pair of legs has pincers. Four other pairs of walking legs. Shell 20–100mm across, although very large ones are not common. Crabs moult their shell as they grow and empty shells often washed up onto beach in large numbers. Scavenger. May be caught using meaty bone.

Velvet swimming crab
Macropipus puber
Length about 80mm. Reddish-brown shell, but covered with muddy-coloured, fine hairs, giving the velvet appearance of its name. Red eyes. First pair of legs with large pincers and last pair of legs have end joint flattened to be used as paddle when swimming. Found under rocks on lower shore and in deeper water.

Beadlet anemone
Actinia equina
Flower-like animal attached to rock. When uncovered by tide, appears as crimson blob of jelly up to about 30mm across and 70mm high. In

water, many tentacles spread out around top of stalk-like body. Mouth in middle of tentacles. Small animals, such as shrimps are stung and killed if they touch these, then pulled in through mouth. May be watched in rock pools.

Dahlia anemone
Tealia felina
Flower-like animal attached to rocks in shaded pools of middle and lower shore. May be up to 50mm across and up to 150mm high when fully stretched. Often covered with pieces of shell and sand, so may not be noticed. Colour varies considerably but tentacles often banded with green, blue, or red.

Common sea urchin
Echinus esculentus
More or less ball-shaped but slightly flattened underneath where mouth is. May be up to 150mm across in really large specimens. Covered with short spines 15mm long. Skeleton, or *test*, made of limy plates fitted together. Deep red with white bumps where reddish spines are fixed. Found on lower shore and in deeper water. Empty tests with spines removed often sold as ornaments. Soft parts are eaten in some countries.

Heart urchin
Echinocardium cordatum
Also called sea potato. Commonly about 50mm long, sometimes larger. Heart-shaped and covered with short, thin spines lying down and pointing towards rear of animal, rather like coarse hair. Yellowish-brown when alive. Burrows in sand. Empty skeleton, or test, may be found on beach. Spines usually rubbed off. Several rows of small holes can then be seen, showing where tube-feet came through test. Other species of heart urchins are different colours, including green or purple.

Common starfish
Asterias rubens
Five arms. Reddish-brown. Up to 250mm across. Rough surface. Underneath each arm is groove containing many tube feet by which starfish moves. Where grooves meet the mouth can be seen. Sometimes found alive in pools, but often washed up on beach by tide. There they are usually stranded and die.

Ragworm
Nereis pelagica
Worm with flattened body made up of many segments with bristles on the sides. Head may be pulled in or pushed out of body and has large, black jaws. Length up to 120mm. Narrows towards the end. Colour a mixture of brown and yellow with thin, red blood-vessel showing clearly along back. Found among rocks and seaweed on lower shore. Other species of ragworms may be green. Fishermen use ragworms as bait.

Lugworm
Arenicola marina
Burrowing worm of sandy and muddy shores. Very much like large earthworm but with gill tufts along fatter front part of body, and often with fleshy ring showing around mouth. Length 100–200mm. Makes U-shaped burrow in the sand with coiled worm cast at surface.

Strandline

Mermaid's purse
Black, oblong, horny case, about 70–100mm long, with a long, curved, stiff point at each corner. This is empty egg-case of common skate. Other species of skates, rays and sharks also lay eggs in similar cases which will vary in size and some may have curled tendrils instead of point.

Egg-case of whelk
Roughly ball-shaped clump of white or cream coloured, papery 'bubbles', each about 8mm wide. The whole mass is 50–100mm across. Each 'bubble' is an empty case in which a whelk egg developed and hatched out when large enough.

Cuttlebone
Oval, flattened, white 'bone'. Made of chalky material and with oval pattern of lines and ridges on surface. Length up to 150mm, or sometimes longer, and about 15–20mm thick in centre. Not a bone at all but the internal shell of the common cuttlefish, *Sepia officinalis*, which falls out when animal dies and decays.

Ammonite
Sometimes called 'snake-stone' because it looks a little like a coiled snake turned to stone. Surface may be smooth, but more often with pattern of ridges or bumps, sometimes both. 15mm–over 1 metre across. Ammonites are the fossilised external shells of an extinct group of animals related to modern squids.

Shipworm-bored wood
Despite its name the shipworm, *Teredo navalis*, is a mollusc and not a worm. The body is long and thin with the two halves of the shell very small and used as a drill for boring into wood such as pier piles and ships' timbers. Mollusc makes lining for tube of chalky substance. Pieces of wood with many borings sometimes washed up.

Belemnite
Looks like a stone bullet. Sometimes brown, but may be grey. Length varies from about 25mm–100mm, and even longer. Belemnites are the fossilised, rod-shaped, internal shell of extinct animals similar in appearance to modern squids.

Herbs

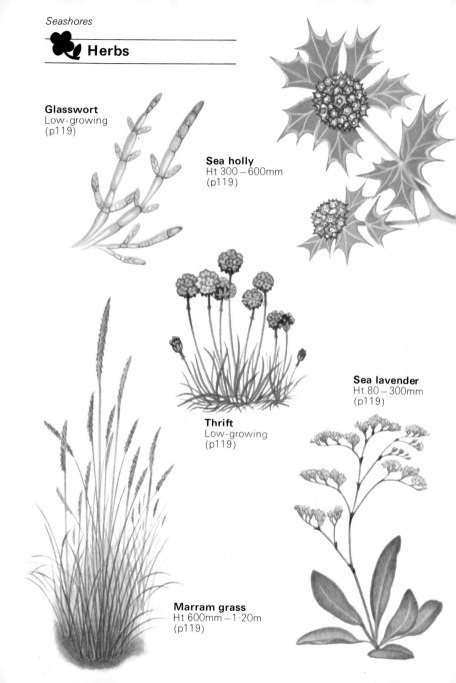

Glasswort
Low-growing
(p119)

Sea holly
Ht 300 – 600mm
(p119)

Thrift
Low-growing
(p119)

Sea lavender
Ht 80 – 300mm
(p119)

Marram grass
Ht 600mm – 1·20m
(p119)

Seaweeds

Toothed wrack
L 600mm
(p119)

Bladderwort
L 150mm – 1m
(p120)

Carragheen
L up to 150mm
(p119)

Oar weed
L 200mm–3m
(p120)

Sea lettuce
L 400 – 500mm
(p120)

Corallina
Ht 50 – 120mm
(p120)

Birds

Common tern
L 350mm
(p120)

Herring gull
L 560mm
(p120)

Great black-backed gull
L 680mm
(p120)

131

Puffin
L 300mm
(p121)

Razorbill
L 400mm
(p121)

Gannet
L 900mm
(p121)

Guillemot
L 400mm
(p121)

Cormorant
L 950mm
(p121)

Avocet
L 425mm
(p121)

Spoonbill
L 860mm
(p121)

Flamingo
L 1·25m
(p121)

Oystercatcher
L 430mm
(p122)

Curlew
L 550mm
(p122)

Shelduck
L 650mm
(p122)

Scoter
L 480mm
(p122)

Dunlin
L 180mm
(p122)

Eider
L 600mm
(p122)

Fish

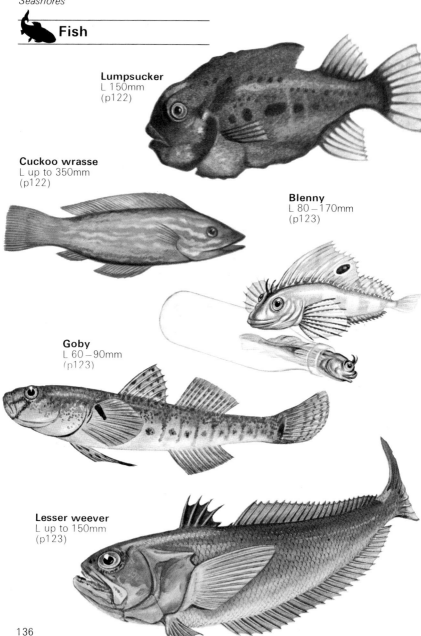

Lumpsucker
L 150mm
(p122)

Cuckoo wrasse
L up to 350mm
(p122)

Blenny
L 80 – 170mm
(p123)

Goby
L 60 – 90mm
(p123)

Lesser weever
L up to 150mm
(p123)

Invertebrates

Limpet
50mm across
(p123)

Periwinkle
Ht 10–20mm
(p123)

Dog whelk
Ht up to 40mm
(p123)

Common whelk
Ht up to 80mm
(p124)

Mussel
L 10–100mm
(p123)

137

Scallop
150mm across
(p124)

Common cockle
30mm across
(p124)

Tellin
L 20mm
(p124)

Razor shell
L up to 150mm
(p124)

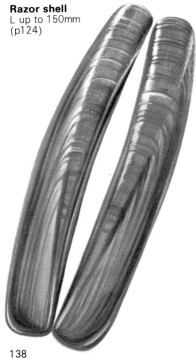

Sand gaper
L up to 120mm
(p124)

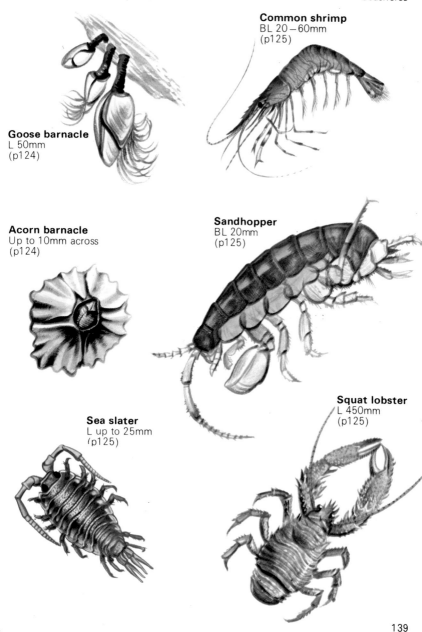

Goose barnacle
L 50mm
(p124)

Common shrimp
BL 20 – 60mm
(p125)

Acorn barnacle
Up to 10mm across
(p124)

Sandhopper
BL 20mm
(p125)

Sea slater
L up to 25mm
(p125)

Squat lobster
L 450mm
(p125)

139

Hermit crab
L up to 120mm
(p125)

Beadlet anemone
Ht 70mm
(p125)

Shore crab
20 – 100mm across
(p125)

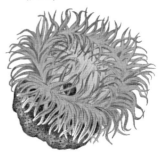

Dahlia anemone
Ht up to 150mm
(p126)

Velvet swimming crab
L 80mm
(p125)

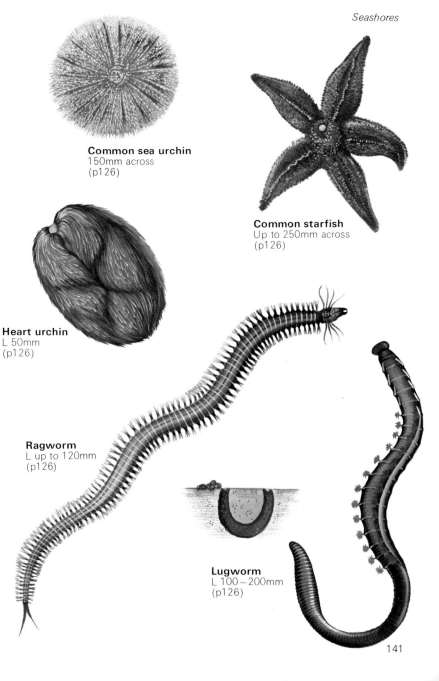

Common sea urchin
150mm across
(p126)

Common starfish
Up to 250mm across
(p126)

Heart urchin
L 50mm
(p126)

Ragworm
L up to 120mm
(p126)

Lugworm
L 100 – 200mm
(p126)

Strandline

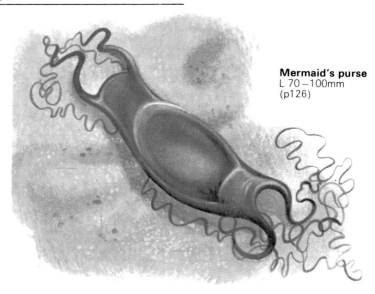

Mermaid's purse
L 70 – 100mm
(p126)

Egg-case of whelk
50 – 100mm across
(p127)

Cuttlebone
L up to 150mm
(p127)

Belemnite
L 25–100mm
(p127)

Ammonite
15mm – 1m across
(p127)

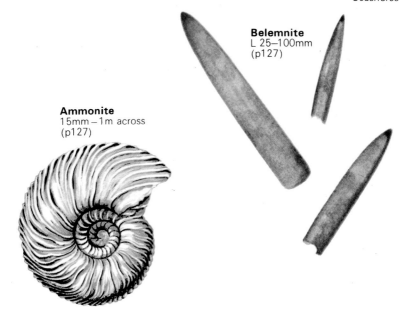

Shipworm-bored wood
(p127)

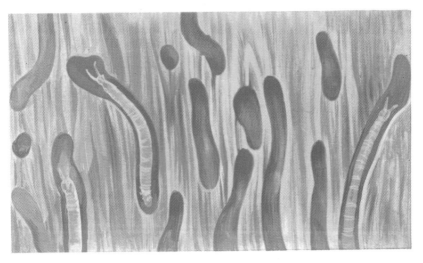

Heaths & Moors

To the bird-watcher, the botanist and the person who likes to be away from crowds, many of the heaths, and even more so the moors, are places of solitude and quietness to be enjoyed. But what makes these places so different from the rest of the countryside?

Heaths are heather-covered lowlands. They are areas of ground where many plants grow, but only those belonging to a few species that are able to cope with the difficult conditions there. The main trouble lies with the soil. A deep hole or trench dug in a heath will show clearly several distinct layers beneath the surface.

Just below the covering of dead pine needles, heather and lichens, lies a thin, dark layer of humus made up of rotted-down plant remains. Below this humus layer, often only a few centimetres thick, can be seen a much thicker layer of ashy-grey sand.

Anyone who has ever tried to fill a moat around a sand castle with water knows that the water simply runs right down into the sand, and a similar thing happens on the heath. The sandy soil cannot hold water close to the surface when it rains, so the rain-water simply drains down through the soil taking with it any useful minerals and humus. Both are essential for plants, so instead of

being in the upper part of the soil where they could be of use, they are deposited much lower down as a dark, yellowish-brown layer, which may become very hard indeed. This process of 'washing-down' is called *leaching*.

Much of the material in the dark layer is made up of iron-containing minerals which cement the sand grains together to form a hard layer often known as the *iron pan*, and

this may sometimes be worth mining for the iron it contains. At one time in England, there was an iron industry in parts of Kent, Surrey and Sussex that depended on the iron mined from the iron pan.

Under the pan is the *bedrock*, that is, the sand or sandstone from which the soil has been made.

As with grassland, heath will only last as long as the tree saplings fail to grow to full size. If that happened, then most heaths, except perhaps those close to the sea, would become first scrub, and then finally woodland. The trees are kept in check by grazing animals such as sheep, goats, or deer, and by deliberate or accidental burning. Occasionally, in the interests of conservation, saplings may even have to be dug up, where there has been no grazing.

Moors are heather-covered uplands. Bleak, wind-swept, wet and lonely, moorland is also grazed by sheep and deer. In Scotland, there are moors where grouse are bred for shooting. These birds feed on young heather, so every few years the moor is set alight to get rid of the old heather and force masses of new heather shoots to spring up.

Yellow gorse covers heathland in summer.

Moors can be bleak, wet and lonely.

On some moors, there are parts where the land is very flat and the rocks below the surface will not allow water to drain away. The ground becomes spongy and wet and a great deal of moss grows. As this dies, it forms peat which builds up into thick layers over the years. These peat bogs often cover large areas and may be dangerous to try and cross. The peat is dug for fuel in some places, and an enormous amount is sold to gardeners to improve their soil.

Life on Heaths & Moors

Heathland, covered with the purple blossom of heather, is common in many parts of the British Isles where the soil is acid and well-drained, and the air is moist. It can also be found in southern Scandinavia, Denmark, north-west Germany, Holland, Belgium and France. Further north, its place is taken by the arctic dwarf scrubland, and in the Mediterranean countries similar dry, scrubby places with evergreen shrubs and trees are known as *mâquis*.

This wild, bushy land is called *mâquis*.

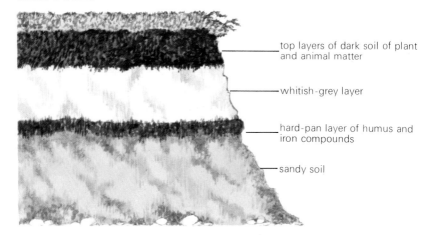

top layers of dark soil of plant and animal matter

whitish-grey layer

hard-pan layer of humus and iron compounds

sandy soil

Poor, sandy heathland soil is unsuitable for most plants other than heather and other shallow-rooted plants. Most roots cannot penetrate the hard-pan layer.

The commonest plant of heathland is heather, or ling. It is able to thrive because it is adapted to living in the dry, sandy soil. Its roots spread out widely only a short distance below the surface so that they are able to absorb rain-water easily, and they are not affected by the hard pan lower down as a plant would be that needed to put down a deep root. Most of the other species on a heath also have shallow root systems.

Once having obtained water, the heather must then make good use of it and not lose it quickly. Plants lose water through tiny holes in the surface of their leaves. It is a normal part of the processes that go on within the plant and where more

water can be taken up from the soil by the plant's roots, there is no problem. But for heathland plants, the loss of large quantities of water in this way would be serious.

To overcome this, the heather has very small leaves, pressed close to the stem so that evaporation from their surface is cut down. Some of the other typical heath plants, such as broom and gorse, have overcome the problem by having fewer leaves. The other work of the leaves, that of making food, has been taken over in these two plants by the green stems. Not completely, perhaps, but to a large degree.

Pine trees also have leaves which are able to reduce evaporation. They are very narrow, so have a small surface. They are tough, and the holes through which the water evaporates lie a little below the surface. This helps to reduce the rate at which the water is lost.

On many heaths, and moors as well, bracken is very common and in some places it may be so plentiful that it kills the heather. Bracken is a fern that spreads by means of underground stems which grow outwards and send up shoots wherever there is room for them. These shoots are very attractive when young. They are green but covered with short, brown hairs and the leaves are curled up in a most interesting way.

Growing on the soil surface, it is usual to find small plants such as various species of mosses and lichens. There may also be small flowering plants on the heath as well as heather. Heath violet and harebell are two that are often found.

In places where the underground water level comes close to the surface and even allows pools of water to form on it, the heath becomes wet and other species of plants may be seen. One, the cross-leaved heath, is similar to heather, but the flowers are a little larger and the small, narrow leaves grow out from the stem in fours, like a cross, which accounts for its name.

The very wet areas have similar plants growing on them to those of the moorland bogs. There may be sphagnum moss, for example, which is able to soak up water like a sponge. If a little is pulled up and squeezed, water will trickle from it.

There may also be butterwort and sundew, which are *insectivorous*, or insect-eating plants. This curious adaptation is necessary because

plants need nitrogen in order to grow properly. Most of them are able to obtain it from the soil, but in these boggy places there may be very little. Now there is also nitrogen in meat and the insectivorous plants get it in this way, from the bodies of small insects.

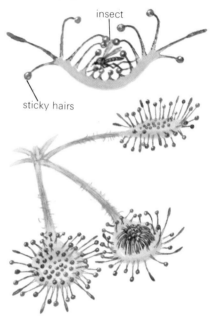

The sundew obtains nitrogen by eating insects.

The sundew has small leaves, round in one species, longer in another. They are covered with small, stiff, red hairs, each with a drop of sticky liquid at the end which looks like dew. The leaves lie flat on the ground as a rosette. Should a small fly, or other insect, walk on a leaf, it will stick; the outer hairs will bend over slowly and trap the insect and juices will ooze from the leaf to dissolve the meat so the plant can absorb it. When only the tough parts are left, the hairs open out again so that the remains can be blown away.

Butterwort has broader, sticky leaves with slightly inrolled edges. Insects that are trapped on the sticky parts are washed by rain to the edges which roll over even more to enclose them so that they can be digested.

On the peaty moors there are likely to be small shrubs. Bilberry is a common one, with its pink flowers that attract the bilberry bumble bee. It has juicy berries later in the year.

The heather of the moors provides food for certain wild animals. Mountain hares depend on it and it is grazed also by red deer. In Scotland, red grouse not only feed on the young shoots, but use it for nesting material also. On some moors, moles are active and short-tailed voles are plentiful, too.

There are plenty of birds to be seen and heard over the moors. Golden plovers, lapwings, meadow pipits and skylarks prefer grassy moorland, but snipe are lovers of wetter places. During the breeding season curlews leave the seashore and come to the moors to nest.

With so many small mammals and birds about, the moor will have predators as well. Foxes are around almost everywhere, and stoats and weasels, too. In some areas wild cats can be found. In the British Isles they live only in Scotland, but they are quite widespread throughout the rest of Europe.

Heathland, rather surprisingly, may have less animal life. There are usually a number of insects to be seen (especially butterflies), but fewer mammals. Birds are quite plentiful, including the Dartford warbler and nightjar and reptiles can sometimes be seen basking. In Britain, dry heaths can often be a haven for adders, the only venomous British snake, and also for smooth snakes which are much rarer.

While the outer layer of a snake's skin is wearing out, a new one is growing underneath. Eventually the snake wriggles out, leaving its old skin behind.

Things to look for on Heaths & Moors

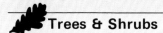
Trees & Shrubs

Scots pine
Pinus sylvestris
Height up to 30 metres. A very common conifer in mountainous places, but also plentiful on heath-land and sandy soil throughout Europe. Old trees have flat top and few branches low down. Bark red or orange on upper part of trunk. Leaves narrow, 30—80mm long, blue-green, in pairs. Cones pea-sized at first, becoming green, pointed and much larger. Seeds escape when cone is over two years old and has turned brown.

Bilberry
Vaccinium myrtillus
Small shrub, up to about 0·5 metres high, but often quite low growing. Twigs green, smooth and ridged. Leaves bright green, oval and point-ed, about 30mm long; drop during the autumn. Flowers small, 4—6mm across, ball-shaped, greenish-pink. Fruit are black berries with purple, powdery appearance and are good to eat from July onwards. Common on heaths and moors throughout Europe. Also called whortleberry and huckle-berry.

Bramble
Rubus fruticosa
Scrambling shrub with very thorny, angled, woody stems. Leaves prickly, usually with three leaflets; toothed edges. Flowers white or pink, 20—30 mm across, with five separate petals. Fruit ('blackberries') with many rounded, fleshy segments, red at first then turning purplish-black when ripe; good to eat. Found on heaths, and many other places such as woods and meadows.

Gorse
Ulex europaeus
Height 0·5—2 metres. Upright shrub furze or whin. Shrub with many blackish branches; *very* spiny. Spines 15—25mm long, grooved. Flowers golden-yellow, smelling of almonds and shaped like pea flowers and some flowers are usually on the plant every month, even in winter. Common on heaths and in rough, grassy places over much of Europe.

Cranberry
Vaccinium oxycoccus
Low growing, creeping, shrub-like plant with thin stems, found growing in bogs and wet heaths. Leaves oval, smooth-edged and pointed tip; dark green above and whitish underneath; 4—8mm long. Flowers small, pale pink, drooping and with four petals turned back. Fruit slightly pear-shaped, spotted with red or brown; rather sharp to the taste and can be used to make a sauce to eat with venison or turkey.

Broom
Sarothamnus scoparius
Height 0·5—2 metres. Upright shrub with many branches. Twigs green, smooth and with ridges along them. Leaves small, oval and pointed; in threes. Flowers golden-yellow, shaped like pea flowers for pollina-tion by large bees. Sometimes con-fused with gorse but absence of spines identifies broom. Common on heaths and in woods where soil is sandy and not chalky at all.

Marsh andromeda
Andromeda polifolia
Also called bog rosemary. Height up to 300mm. Shrub with small, smooth, upright stems with few branches. Leaves narrow-oval with smooth

edges, pointed, dark green above, whitish underneath. Flowers in small clusters at end of stem; stalked, nodding, pink, well-rounded, 5–7mm across, often visited by bumble-bees and butterflies. Found on bogs and wet heaths mainly in northern and central Europe.

 Herbs

Purple moor-grass
Molinia caerulea
Height 300mm–1·5 metres. A very common grass in damp or wet, peaty places. Leaves long and narrow, gradually ending in a fine point. They die down each year. Flowers form plumes at end of a tall stalk and vary in colour from dark purple to brown, yellow or green. Plant forms large tussocks in damp heaths and on mountains. Not found in far south of Europe.

Ling
Calluna vulgaris
Height up to 600mm. Tough, shrubby evergreen with many branched and twisted stems. Leaves very small, 1–2mm long, lying close to stem. Flowers small, pale purple. Very common and plentiful on heaths and moors throughout Europe and is often the most abundant plant present. Also commonly called heather.

Cross-leaved heath
Erica tetralix
Height up to 600mm. Short, shrubby plant with branching and often twisted stems. Leaves small, narrow, 2–4mm long and attached to stem *in fours.* Flowers in small bunches of four to twelve, hanging down at top of a stem, each one fairly rounded but small at the mouth; rose-pink. Grows on wet heaths and moors, mainly in western Europe.

Harebell
Campanula rotundifolia
Height 150–400mm. A slender, delicate looking plant that grows on dry, shallow and sandy soil. Stem thin and smooth. Leaves nearest roots are stalked and roundish. Leaves on stem are narrow and pointed. Flowers about 15mm long and hang down on thin stalks; blue but sometimes white, bell-shaped with pointed lobes around mouth. Also called bluebell in Scotland, but should not be confused with English bluebell, *Endymion nonscriptus*.

Cotton-grass
Eriophorum angustifolium
Height 200–600mm. Not really a grass at all, but leaves are long and narrow like grass. Spreads by underground, creeping stems. Flowerstalks upright with three to seven brown, scaly, nodding flower-heads at top. When fruits are formed, they have long, fine, white hairs to help carry them long distances and masses of these at top of each stalk look like tufts of white cotton-wool. Grows in wet bogs.

Butterwort
Pinguicula vulgaris
Height 50–150mm. Insect-eating plant found in bogs and wet heaths. Leaves 20–80mm long, more or less oblong, yellow-green, curled at edges, sticky and hairy, forming a rosette lying against the ground. Flowers growing from centre of rosette, each on the end of thin, smooth stalk; purple with white patch at throat and long spur. Insects are washed to edges of leaves where they are digested.

Tormentil
Potentilla erecta
Creeping plant, very common on heaths and moors where soil is not heavy or chalky. Stems thin,

branched and covered with fine, short hairs. Leaves appear to be made up of five leaflets, with large teeth along edges and pointed tip. No roots grow from trailing stems. Flowers 7—11mm across, with four more or less heart-shaped petals, and showing green sepals between them.

Bog asphodel
Narthecium ossifragum
Height up to 400mm. Found in wet places. Leaves near roots upright, often slightly curved, stiff, 50—300 mm high but only 2—5mm wide. Flower stems upright with few small, narrow leaves. Very attractive star-like flowers, golden yellow with five, narrow, pointed petals. Once thought to make bones of animals brittle if they ate the plants and this is shown by the *ossifragum* part of the name which means 'bone-breaking'.

Sheep's bit
Jasione montana
Height 50—500mm. Slightly hairy plant with stems that may lie along ground for short way before turning upwards. Leaves about 50mm long, narrow, fairly pointed and with wavy edges. Flowers small, blue, with narrow, pointed lobes; many of them close together as slightly flattened, rounded mass, 5—35mm across, at top of stalk. Found on heaths and grassy places where there is sandy soil or where there is no chalk.

Milkwort
Polygala vulgaris
Low growing plant but with some stems 100—300mm high, found on heaths and grassy parts of moors. Leaves long-oval, smooth edges, pointed, not opposite each other on stem. Many flowers along upper part of stem; usually blue, but also pink or white. Gets the name milkwort from the once-held belief that animals which fed on it gave more milk.

Sundew
Drosera rotundifolia
Height 60—250mm. Insect-eating plant growing in wet, peaty places on heaths and moors in most of Europe except around Mediterranean. Leaves form rosette against ground. Each leaf round, up to 10mm across, with long, narrow stalk; reddish tinge; covered with red, sticky hairs for trapping insects. Flowers small, white.

Hard fern
Blenchum spicant
Height 100—750mm. Common fern of heaths and moors except where there is chalk or limestone. Fronds grow in tufts. Outer ones have 30—60 lobes on either side of main stalk and look like double-sided combs. Inner fronds are slightly longer and lobes have spore-cases on undersides.

Sphagnum moss
Species of Sphagnum
There are several different species of sphagnum moss and they all grow in wet, boggy places. Plants grow in thick masses. Stems long and thin with many leafy branches in rosettes, giving the moss a shaggy appearance. Leaves are able to absorb large amounts of water. Lower parts of moss rot and form peat which is dug for fuel in some moorland places.

Club moss
Lycopodium clavatum
Sometimes called stag's-horn moss. Long, creeping stems, 300mm—1 metre, branching and most of them lying along ground. Leaves small, 3—5mm, narrow and pointed with hair-like tips, arranged in spirals around stem and lying close against it; bright green. Some branches slender and upright and these have one or two cones on the end. Each cone 20—50mm long, with sharp-pointed leaves covering tiny, bean-

shaped spore cases. Spores form bright yellow powder.

Lichens

Simple plants. Many different species on heaths and moors, some forming crusty patches on rocks and trees, some hanging like coarse, blue-grey hair. Worth looking for are those that grow on the ground, about 30mm high, or less; blue-grey or greyish-green, like tiny clubs with bright red tops. Another kind is like very small, stalked cups.

 Birds

Golden eagle
Aquila chrysaetos
Length of female 910mm (slightly larger than male). A large bird of mountains and moorland. Almost completely brown with a golden sheen on head and back of neck. Soars when searching for food which may be mountain hares, large birds, lambs or carrion. Huge wings with span of over 2 metres. Nests on crag or pine tree and same nest used year after year, sticks being added each time.

Hobby
Falco subbuteo
Length 275–300mm. Bird of prey, which may be quite common over many European heaths, but not in much of Scandinavia. Grey back; black 'moustache' and under eyes; white breast, heavily streaked with black; red thighs. In flight very pointed wings and rather short tail can be easily seen. Excellent flier, able to twist and turn easily to catch large insects, small birds and bats.

Hen harrier
Circus cyaneus
Length 425–510mm. Bird of prey. Female has dark brown back,

streaked underparts, bare across tail. Male grey with white underparts, black wing-tips. Nests on moorland. Hunts by gliding low over ground looking for voles and other small creatures. Long tail well seen in flight, and wings held as open V. Northern birds migrate southwards in winter, even to north Africa.

Buzzard
Buteo buteo
Length 500–525mm. Colour varies but commonly dark brown back; bars across tail; pale underparts with brown streaks. A bird of prey, often seen soaring over moors, searching for small mammals which are its main food. Will also eat lizards, beetles and carrion. Makes large nest of sticks in tree or a rocky ledge.

Meadow pipit
Anthus pratensis
Length 150mm. Common on heaths and lowland moors. Dull brown upper parts with darker brown markings; breast whiter and streaked. Small, narrow, pointed beak. Nest of grass lined with hair, on ground. Often victim of cuckoo. Northern birds migrate south in winter.

Dartford warbler
Sylvia undata
Length 125mm. Back dark brown; head grey; underparts dark red; long tail which it flicks. Small bird, rare in England where it lives on heaths of some southern counties among gorse bushes. Much more common in dry areas around the Mediterranean and north-west Europe. Eats insects and spiders. Nests among gorse or heather and decorates nest with spiders' webs.

Cuckoo
Cuculus canorus
Length 325mm. Most cuckoos have grey head, back and tail and barred underparts. Some females, however,

are brown rather than grey. Best known for its song of 'cuckoo' repeated over and over again. Lays eggs in nests of other birds, usually meadow pipit, dunnock or reed warbler. Young cuckoos looked after by foster parent. Found throughout Europe in places with bushes and hedges, but also moorland.

Hooded crow
Corvus corone cornix
Length 450mm. Very similar in size and shape to carrion crow, but easily recognised by grey back and underparts. Found over much of Europe, but not in Spain. Eats carrion, insects and eggs and chicks of other birds. Hated by game-keepers because it may take young game birds. So closely related to carrion crow that it may interbreed in some areas.

Nightjar
Caprimulgus europaeus
Length 267mm. Night-flying, insect-eating bird. Colour various shades of brown for camouflage. Male has white spots near wing-tips. Flattish head; bristles around mouth. Eyes very wide open at night but just slits in daytime. Spends day on ground or branches. Very difficult to see as markings make it look like dead leaves. Makes churring trill as it flies.

Linnet
Acanthis cannabina
Length 125mm. Common on heaths. Male has brown back; white wing bar; forked tail with white sides; crimson on breast and top of head in summer and some may remain in winter. Female similar but without red. May nest in groups, close to ground in bushes. Northern birds may migrate further south in winter.

Greenshank
Tringa nebularia
Length 300mm. Grey above with darker grey markings; white under-

parts with dark spots on throat and breast. Small head; long grey beak, slightly upturned. Long green legs. Seen in winter along coasts and marshes, but nests on moors in Britain and northern Europe. Nest is a scrape on ground.

Red grouse
Lagopus lagopus
Length 325–375mm. Heavy-bodied bird, rather like a chicken. Short wings. Reddish-brown with darker wings and tail. Male has bright red 'eyebrows'. Mainly ground-living bird, feeding on heather shoots. Flies short distances with fast wing-beats which make a whirring sound. Red grouse found only in Britain, but very similar to willow grouse found over much of northern Europe.

Lapwing
Vanellus vanellus
Length 300mm. Also known as peewit from its call. Dark glossy green back, head and throat, appearing black unless sun is shining on it; white beneath. Fairly long legs. Very common in fields and on moors, in flocks. During breeding season may roll and twist in the air. Easy to recognise in flight by black and white pattern and rounded wings. Slender crest on head.

Black grouse
Lyrurus tetrix
Length of male 525mm, female smaller. Lives on heaths and moors, and also in birch woods in winter, over much of northern and eastern Europe. Male glossy, blue-black; white wing-bar; red 'eyebrows'; outward-curling tail feathers (usually called 'lyre-shaped'), white underneath. Females speckled brown; forked tail. At start of breeding season, males display on special areas called *leks*. Males are known as blackcocks, females as greyhens.

Golden plover
Pluvialis apricaria
Length 275mm. In summer, golden brown and speckled upper parts; black below. In winter the black disappears and underparts are light-coloured. Nests on moors. Found along western edge of Europe and Scandinavia but becoming scarcer in some parts, especially Britain. In winter it leaves moors and goes to mud-flats and fields where it may join flocks of lapwings.

Ring ouzel
Turdus torquatus
Length 240mm. Belongs to blackbird family and very similar in appearance. Male black with broad, white collar across breast. Female browner with less well-marked white band. Nests on ground or close to it, and often not far from a stream. In summer found in Norway, parts of Britain and highlands of southern Europe.

Raven
Corvus corax
Length over 630mm. Large all-black bird with big, strong beak. Similar to rook and crow but much bigger. Common only in wild and lonely places, and not at all in France and much of Germany. During courtship, ravens may tumble about in the air and show off their flying skill. Feeds on almost anything, but especially carrion.

 Mammals

Sheep
Sheep kept on moors for grazing must be very hardy. Most of them are smaller and more active than those in more sheltered lowland areas. They are bred for their meat, but their wool is used for carpets, clothing and knitting wool. There are several hill-breeds and common ones in Britain are Cheviot, Welsh Mountain, Swaledale and Blackface. Some breeds are horned, but others are hornless.

Mountain hare
Lepus timidus
Body length 570–610mm, tail 50–65mm. Mountain, or blue, hare found in Scotland, Ireland, Scandinavia and the Alps. Smaller than brown hare and with shorter ears. Summer coat brown; white tail; black tips to ears. Coat turns white in winter, but black ear tips remain. Often seen during the day. Lays up in the shelter of rocks.

Short-tailed vole
Microtus agrestis
Body length 95–133mm, tail 27–46 mm. Rather long-haired; darker than many of the voles. Often seen during day-time. Makes underground burrows and in winter will burrow under the snow. Makes ball-shaped nest above ground. Found on rough meadows and moorland throughout most of northern Europe, not in southern countries.

 **Reptiles**

Smooth snake
Coronella austriaca
Length up to 600mm. The smooth snake is so-called because the scales have no ridges and are perfectly smooth. Greyish-brown or reddish, with black spots along back and sides. Sides may be whitish. In England, found only in a few areas in the south, but it is one of the commonest snakes in central Europe. Not venomous. Eats lizards and small mammals.

Adder
Vipera berus
Length up to 800mm. Females larger than males. Common snake of dry heathlands, often seen basking in

sun. Colour varies and may be grey, green, or even almost black, but always with dark, zig-zag pattern along back. Feeds mostly on mice, young birds and lizards, which are killed by venom injected by adder when it bites. May bite humans in self-defence, which is painful; wound should be treated by doctor quickly, but is rarely fatal.

 **Invertebrates**

Large heath butterfly
Coenonympha tullia
Wingspan 31–37mm. Found on upland moors. Colour and pattern may vary. Upper surface of wings reddish-brown with dark spot and pale ring around it on fore-wings. Hind wings may have several spots. Underside of wings have light bar across them. Hind wings are partly dull greenish-brown. Fore and hind wings with spots. Caterpillar green with pale stripes and feeds on grasses and sedges.

Green hairstreak butterfly
Callophrys rubi
Wingspan 25mm. Small butterfly. Upper surface of wings brown. Underside dull green with narrow white streak across hind wings. Found along the edge of woods, over downs, heaths and moors. Caterpillar green and feeds on a number of plants such as gorse, bramble and rock rose.

Emperor moth
Saturnia pavonia
Wingspan 55–75mm. Large moth and Britain's only silk moth, although the silk is of no value. Fore-wings grey with bands and patches of white and brown. 'Eye' markings large. Hind wings orange-brown with dark band near hind edges; also have 'eye' markings. Female larger than male. Found on heathland. Eggs laid on heather and bramble. Caterpillar green with black rings and yellow spots.

Wood ant
Formica rufa
Length 9mm. Found on heathland among pine trees, as well as in pine woods. Nest looks like a heap of swept-up pine needles, sometimes nearly a metre high. Worker ants can usually be seen scurrying to and fro collecting food. Queen stays inside nest. Workers not only build nest and find food, but look after eggs and larvae. Body reddish-brown in front, but almost black at rear.

Crab spider
Thomisus onustus
Length 8mm. Bright pink with two cone-shaped bumps on body. Well-camouflaged and difficult to see when hiding among flowers of bell-heather. Keeps very still until an insect comes to the flower; then seizes it. During summer female guards egg-sac which is fixed to heather shoots. Many species of spiders can be found on heaths.

Trees & Shrubs

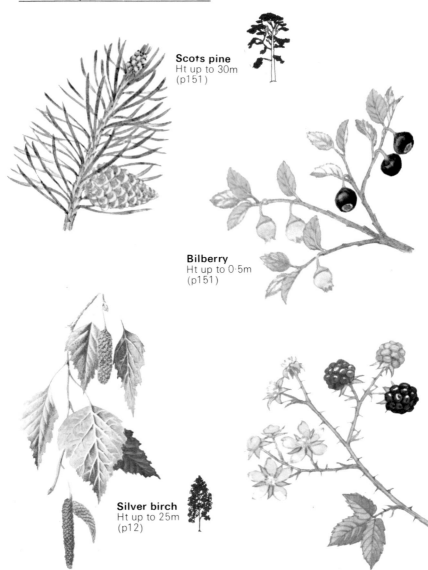

Scots pine
Ht up to 30m
(p151)

Bilberry
Ht up to 0·5m
(p151)

Silver birch
Ht up to 25m
(p12)

Gorse
Ht 0·5–2m
(p151)

Cranberry
Low-growing
(p151)

Bramble
Scrambling
(p151)

Broom
Ht 0.5 – 2m
(p151)

Marsh andromeda
Ht up to 300mm
(p151)

 Herbs

Ling
Ht up to 600mm
(p152)

Purple moor-grass
Ht 300mm—1·5m
(p152)

Cross-leaved heath
Ht up to 600mm
(p152)

Harebell
Ht 150 – 400mm
(p152)

Butterwort
Ht 50 – 150mm
(p152)

Cotton-grass
Ht 200 – 600mm
(p152)

Tormentil
Creeping
(p152)

Bog asphodel
Ht up to 400mm
(p153)

Milkwort
Low-growing
(p153)

Sheep's bit
Ht 50 – 500mm
(p153)

Sundew
H: 60–250mm
(p153)

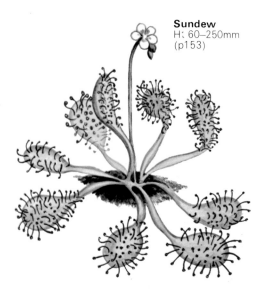

Bracken
Ht up to 2m
(p15)

Violet
Ht 20 – 200mm
(p13)

Hard fern
Ht 100 – 750mm
(p153)

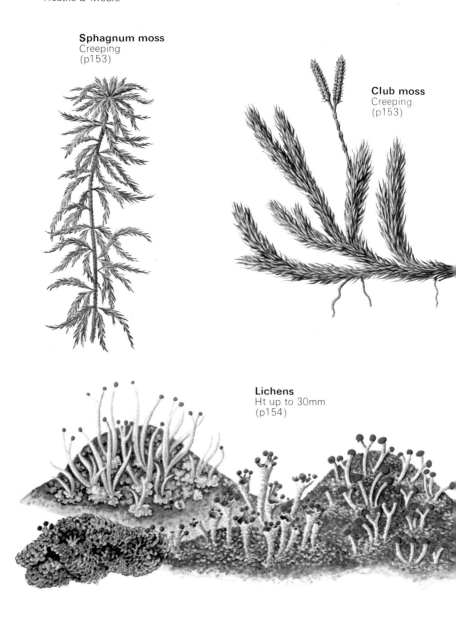

Sphagnum moss
Creeping
(p153)

Club moss
Creeping
(p153)

Lichens
Ht up to 30mm
(p154)

Birds

Hen harrier
L 425–510mm
(p154)

Golden eagle
L (f) 910mm
(p154)

Hobby
L 275–300mm
(p154)

Buzzard
L 500–525mm
(p154)

Meadow pipit
L 150mm
(p154)

Dartford warbler
L 125mm
(p154)

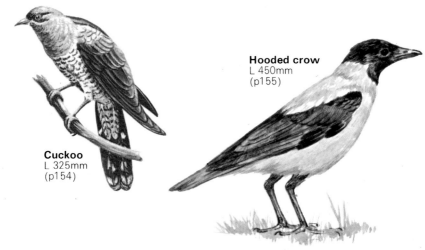

Hooded crow
L 450mm
(p155)

Cuckoo
L 325mm
(p154)

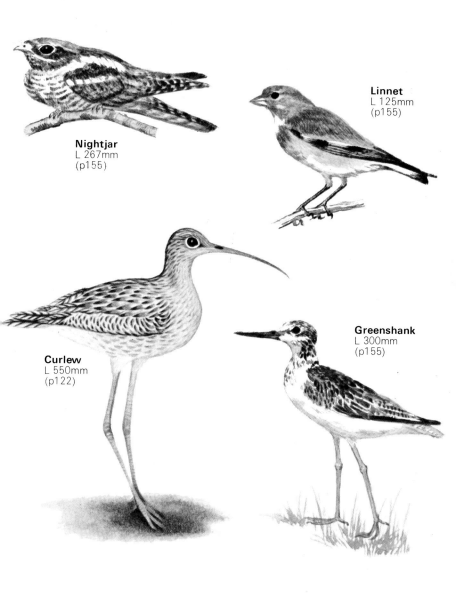

Nightjar
L 267mm
(p155)

Linnet
L 125mm
(p155)

Curlew
L 550mm
(p122)

Greenshank
L 300mm
(p155)

Red grouse
L 325 – 375mm
(p155)

Black grouse
L (m) 525mm
(p155)

Lapwing
L 300mm
(p155)

Golden plover
L 275mm
(p156)

Skylark
L 180mm
(p53)

Ring ouzel
L 240mm
(p156)

Raven
L 630mm
(p156)

Mammals

Cheviot
(p156)

Welsh Mountain
(p156)

Swaledale
(p156)

Blackface
(p156)

Red deer
BL 1·75 — 2·5m
(p19)

Red fox
BL 580 – 770mm
(p19)

Stoat
BL 220 – 290mm
(p56)

Weasel
BL 210 – 230mm
(p56)

Wild cat
BL 475 – 800mm
(p20)

Mountain hare
BL 570 – 610mm
(p156)

Rabbit
BL 340 – 455mm
(p56)

Short-tailed vole
BL 95 – 133mm
(p156)

Mole
BL 115 – 150mm
(p56)

Reptiles

Smooth snake
L up to 600mm
(p156)

Adder
L up to 800mm
(p156)

Invertebrates

Large heath butterfly
Ws 31 – 37mm
(p157)

Emperor moth
Ws 55–75mm
(p157)

Green hairstreak butterfly
Ws 25mm
(p157)

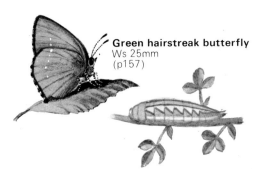

Crab spider
L 8mm
(p157)

Wood ant
L 9mm
(p157)

Mountains

Europe has many mountains, ranging from the high, pointed peaks of the Alps, to the lower, more rounded mountains of Scotland. The difference in appearance between them is due largely to their age. Those high, pointed alpine peaks are very young, geologically speaking; only about fifty million years have passed since they were formed, whereas some of the Scottish mountains were pushed up much further back in the mists of time, as much as 400 million years. These old mountains, not only those of Scotland, but of Norway and the Black Forest region in Germany, too, may look quite rugged in places, but they are really only worn-down stumps. Given time, the Alps will come to look like them, but by then the older mountains will have been worn away completely.

The Alps extend into several countries, including Switzerland, France and Austria. Large rivers

An alpine lake in winter.

run through them and among their peaks are to be found a number of large glaciers which are slow-moving rivers of ice. A great deal of ice has been made in the Alps, and in the past its movement has widened and deepened many of the valleys. This has not been the case with the Pyrenees, the mountains of the French and Spanish border. Although the same age as the Alps, the valleys are much narrower and show that they have not been affected by ice in the same way.

Mountains can be cold places and as you climb, the temperature falls about 1 °C for every 500 metres higher that you go. This means that the summits of some of the high mountains will be so cold that they will always be covered in snow. The change in temperature with height will affect the plants that grow there, and several *zones* will be passed through during a climb up a mountain.

Low down is the broad-leaved forest zone and it is here that you will find most of the towns and villages. Higher up, the temperature becomes too cold for the broad-leaves and the coniferous forest becomes the main vegetation zone. In some places, the trees have been cleared and in the higher parts, the forests may open out into meadows.

There comes a point, however, where trees are unable to grow easily because of the low temperatures. This is the *tree line* and above this is the alpine zone, rich in small flowering plants, shrubs and lichens.

Despite this general fall in temperature with height, conditions may vary tremendously within a small area. The sun may shine on one side of a valley and make it quite warm, yet the other side will remain in shadow and be bitterly cold. Even two sides of the same

rock may show a considerable difference in temperature for the same reason. These variations will obviously affect the plant and animal life a great deal.

The effect of frost and ice will be to crack rocks and form crevices just large enough for plants to grow in. Many small pieces of rock will break off larger ones and in some places large areas of rock fragments, known as *screes* will be formed. Even these will have their own particular species of plants growing on them.

Mountainous countries sometimes have beautiful lakes. Cold and crystal-clear, some, like those of the Italian Alps, are very deep. Many of these lakes contain fish that are able to live in these cold waters and these in turn, may attract certain birds.

A diagram showing the various zones of a mountain range.

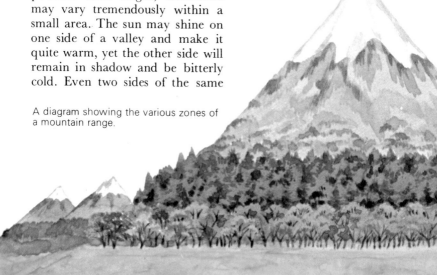

Life on Mountains

The different vegetation zones in mountains will contain their own particular animal populations. These will also vary in different parts of Europe, often depending on whether or not man has hunted there.

In the coniferous forests of all the mountainous regions there are a number of birds rarely seen in other habitats. These forests consist of pine trees, spruce and larch. They all bear cones which contain seeds, and crossbills are birds that have become adapted for feeding on pine seeds. As their name suggests, the tips of the top and bottom parts of the beak are crossed which makes it easier for the birds to pick out the seeds from the cones.

Woodpeckers inhabit these forests also, but not all the species live in the same part. This is usual in the animal world. Where more than one closely related species occupy the same kind of habitat, they do not compete for the same food supply and they are usually found looking for slightly different kinds of food or else in a different part of the habitat.

The greater spotted woodpecker is more often heard than seen and its fast drumming on the wood is very difficult to trace. The largest species in Europe is the black woodpecker, which does not occur in Britain.

Mammals of these forests include the beautiful pine marten which is found throughout most of Europe, but is becoming much rarer. The largest carnivore to be found in Europe is the brown bear. This is now very rare and only a few still live in the Dolomites and the Pyrenees. Another carnivore, the lynx, still exists in small numbers in the forests of north-east and central Europe, but the smaller Spanish lynx now survives only in parts of Spain and southern Europe and is possibly one of the world's rarest mammals.

The meadows of the mountain regions are a delight for anyone interested in flowers, and are one of the many pleasant sights that visitors to Switzerland and Austria remember. These meadows occur where the coniferous forests begin to

permanent snow zone

snow line

5,050m

alpine zone

tree line

3,800m

coniferous forest

3,200m

deciduous forest

2,600m

Alpine meadows are a delight in spring.

open out, and also just above the tree line. Flowering plants are plentiful, including the small, shrubby alpine rhododendron in the higher meadows and many species of orchid in the lower ones. A number of the meadow plants are protected and it is against the law to pick them. Many of the lower meadows are grazed, or cut for hay.

Well above the tree line in the alpine zone, the plants include small shrubs, mosses and lichens. There are other flowering plants but many of them will be dwarf cushions, such as the saxifrages. Some plants will have gained a root-hold in crevices, while others will have found a suitable spot by a mountain spring.

For much of the year, the ground in the alpine zone will be covered with snow. When the snow melts, there will be plenty of moisture but the summer will be short, so the plants will need to grow, flower and produce their seeds quickly before the snow falls again. Very few plants are able to grow where the snow is permanent, only simple plants such as algae and lichens, or an occasional flowering plant like the ice crowfoot.

There are few mammals that live in the alpine zone. Those that do include mountain hares and alpine marmots. Marmots are burrowing animals that live between 1000 and 3000 metres above sea-level. They live in colonies wherever the soil is deep enough for their burrows. While they are feeding, one marmot will act as a sentry to warn the others with a whistle if there is any danger. When autumn arrives, the marmots close the entrance to their burrows and hibernate through the winter, reappearing when the snow melts in spring.

Among the animals that live in places where winter snow is always present, it is common for them to develop white fur during the winter months for camouflage. Mountain hares do this. They are found throughout much of Europe and now and again they appear in the Alps.

Of the few larger species of mammals that can exist high up in the mountains, the one most likely to be seen is the chamois. It is very sure-footed and can jump over wide crevasses and land on a small ledge on the other side without slipping. It can bound up steep, rocky, mountain slopes without any difficulty, finding footholds where none seem to be. As winter approaches, the herds of chamois are forced down to the woods. In fact, they may even stay there all the year round if they are not disturbed.

The ibex is another animal of the mountains. It was once hunted so much that it became almost extinct. However, in north-west Italy there is an alpine area which was made into a national park in 1922 and the animals in it were strictly protected. The numbers of ibex there increased and recently it has been possible to trap some and take them to the mountains of Switzerland, Austria and Germany where they have been released.

Alpine birds include the alpine chough which feeds upon berries and small creatures that it finds in rock crevices. There are small finches and warblers, but possibly the most exciting birds to see are the larger birds of prey, the golden eagle and the lammergeyer. This last bird has come close to extinction and the last remaining ones in Europe now live only in the Spanish mountains. The lammergeyer feeds on carrion and if any bones are too large for it to manage, it will soar up with one in its beak and drop it onto the rocks below, where it will break into pieces small enough for the bird to cope with.

In the areas where there are large lakes, fish are plentiful. There may

A few animals found in mountain ranges.

be lake trout, char, grayling and whitefish (a name used for several very similar kinds of fish). Of course, where there are fish, there will also be fish-eating birds, and herons are a common sight. Now and again around the northern lakes the osprey may be seen swooping down to the water to catch fish in its sharp talons.

Things to look for on Mountains

 Trees & Shrubs

Silver fir
Abies alba
Pyramid-shaped conifer up to 50 metres high. Bark silvery-grey, smooth at first but becoming cracked and rough later. Leaves very narrow, 15–30mm long, flattened, each with small notch at the end. Cones quite large, 100–160mm long, standing upright on branches. When ripe, scales and seeds fall from cones, leaving the centre stalk still in position. Silver fir forms forests in mountains of central and southern Europe.

Mountain pine
Pinus mugo
Sometimes small tree, but more often a straggling bush. Has short, thick, straight trunk and low growing branches. Height up to 3.5 metres. Grows high up on mountains of central and southern Europe up to 2400–2700 metres, sometimes growing above the usual limit for trees. Leaves like needles, 30–80mm long, in pairs, stiff and curved. Scales of cones have bumps of various sizes on them.

Dwarf juniper
Juniperus communis nana
Height 100–150mm. A very low growing shrub, dense and spreading like a mat over ground. Leaves 4–8mm long, 2mm wide suddenly narrowing to a point, lying close to stem and may be turned up. Fruit green at first turning bluish-black when ripe. Grows on dry ground and stony slopes up to 3570 metres in Alps, Pyrenees and Appenines. Grows higher up than any other woody plant in Europe.

Alpine rhododendron
Rhododendron ferrugineum
Also called Alpenrose. Height up to 1 metre. Small, evergreen shrub growing on mountain pastures and among rocks between 1500–2800 metres. Much-branched. Leaves dark green above but look rusty underneath because of the covering of small, brown hairs; rolled at the edges. Flowers bright pinkish-red, about 20mm long, in clusters at end of stem.

Mezereon
Daphne mezereon
Height 0.5–1 metre. Upright shrub without many branches. Clusters of purple, sweet-scented flowers, 8–12 mm across, appear on stems before leaves open. Leaves 40–100mm long; long-oval. Fruit are scarlet, fleshy and poisonous. Grows in woods up to the stony pastures. Alpine mezereon with white flowers, grows higher up on rocks.

Alpine rose
Rosa pendulina
Small, shrub, 0.5–2 metres high, found in shady places on mountains, often in woods. Branches reddish with few prickles, often none. Leaves made up of several oval, toothed, leaflets on main stalk, dark green and covered with fine hairs. Petals bright pink; flowers 35–50mm across. Fruit bright red, oval, narrowing to a 'neck'.

 Herbs

Gentian
Species of *Gentiana*
Low growing herbs, often about 50–100mm high, found growing in mountain meadows, stony places or

among rocks. Leaves of some species narrow, others oval. Flowers funnel-shaped with spreading lobes and commonly a very beautiful blue colour. Some may be purple, or white. The illustration on page 193 shows a non-European species commonly grown in rock gardens.

Yellow wolf's bane
Aconitum vulparia
Upright, branching plant, 0·5–1 metre high. Leaves deeply divided into several narrow, toothed lobes. Flowers on upper part of stems where it is leafless. Each flower on short stalk, pale yellow with tall, narrow hood about three times as long as wide. Found in mountain woods and damp meadows. Poisonous.

Alpine trefoil
Trifolium alpinum
Height 50–200mm. Spreading plant with upright flowering stems. Leaves have three leaflets, long-oval, 10–15mm in length. Flowers quite long, about 20mm, shaped like pea flowers, rosy-purple, three to twelve of them in cluster at end of stem. Grows in meadows and stony places up to 3100 metres in Alps, Pyrenees and northern Appenines.

Wild pink
Dianthus plumarius
Height up to 400mm. Grows in tufts. Leaves narrow and stiff, sharply pointed, with a bluish-grey powdery appearance. Flowers 25–35mm across, pink or white, with petals cut half-way down into narrow, feathery lobes. Sweet-scented. Grows wild on mountains but is cultivated a great deal.

Fragrant orchid
Gymnadenia conopsea
Height 150–400mm. Common orchid of alpine meadows and edges of woods up to 2450 metres. Leaves narrow and long, upper ones nar-

rower than lower. Flowers about 10mm across, pinkish-red, with petals forming lip and hood. Spur about 12mm long. Many flowers along upper part of stem. Found in most mountain areas of Europe.

Monkshood
Aconitum napellus
Height 0·5–1 metre. Leaves divided into narrow lobes right to mid-rib. Each lobe further divided into smaller, narrow, toothed lobes. Flowers deep blue or bluish-purple with a high hood. Many flowers clustered along upper part of stem. Found in damp meadows and woods up to 2000 metres in parts of Alps. *A very poisonous plant.*

Orange hawkweed
Hiercacium aurantiacum
Height 200–500mm. Most of the leaves as a rosette against the ground; long, narrow, oval, dark green, hairy. Few smaller leaves on stem. Stem unbranched except at top where there are short stalks to carry the flowers. Flower-heads brick-red, about 15mm across shaped like dandelion flower-heads; one to six of them in a cluster. Found in mountain meadows and among rocks, up to 2600 metres throughout most of Europe. Also called Grim the Collier and Devil's paintbrush.

Stemless carline thistle
Carlina acaulis
Height up to 300mm. Leaves long, up to 300mm, lobed with spines on them, lying close to ground as a rosette. Flower-head 50–130mm across, usually without a stem but occasionally with one up to 300mm high; white or reddish and surrounded with a ring of silvery-white, papery *bracts* which close up together when the air is damp, and open when it is dry. Grows in meadows and stony places up to 2800 metres over much of Europe.

Edelweiss
Leontopodium alpinum
Height 50–200mm. Leaves long-oval, upper ones smaller than lower; greenish but covered with white hairs giving them a grey appearance. Stem upright, thin, with two to ten yellow flower-heads clustered at top and surrounded by six to nine narrow leaves, densely woolly and white, spreading out like a star. A very well-known alpine plant of pastures and rocky places of central Europe. Sometimes called flannel-flower.

Musky saxifrage
Saxifraga moschata
Height 25–75mm. Low growing plant. Makes cushions of tightly-packed, short shoots. Leaves 3–15mm long, deeply divided in rosettes. Flower-stems up to 100mm, with small oval leaves and from one to seven flowers. Flowers white or pale yellow, 8mm across. Grows on rocks and piles of rock fragments, high up in mountains of central and eastern Alps. There are many different species of saxifrage.

Spiked bell-flower
Campanula spicata
Height 200mm–1 metre. Leaves strap-shaped with blunt point; hairy; most of them near base of stem and some forming a rosette on ground. Easy to recognise because of the tall stem with many stalkless flowers clustered along the upper half of it. Flowers bluish or purple, bell-shaped, with pointed lobes. Grows in meadows and on stony slopes in Alps and Apennines. Many species of bell-flower may be found on mountains.

Spring anemone
Pulsatilla vernalis
Height 50–150mm. Leaves evergreen and made up of several toothed, three-lobed leaflets on hairy stem. Single flower on end of hairy stem with several feathery leaves just below it. Flower cup-shaped, 40–60mm across, nodding at first and then upright. Petals white, but tinged with pink or violet, hairy on the outside. Many golden-yellow stamens clustered inside. Grows in meadows and stony places. Flowers early, often as the snow is melting.

Moss campion
Silene acaulis
Height 50mm. Very low-growing, creeping plant, forming bright green cushions on damp rocks and in cracks high up on mountains. Leaves 6–12 mm long, narrow, hairy edges, in rosettes. Flowers only 9–12mm across, on short stalk 20–100mm high. Petals pink, reddish, or occasionally white, and notched at the end.

Mountain buttercup
Ranunculus montanus
Height 160–300mm. Similar to meadow buttercup of the lowlands. Larger leaves have three to five toothed lobes and smaller upper leaves on stem are strap-shaped. Flowers golden-yellow, 200–300mm across. Grows in meadows, woods and on mountains up to 2800 metres in Alps, Pyrenees and Apennines.

Ice crowfoot
Ranunculus glacialis
Low growing, rather hairy plant of buttercup family. Leaves lobed and toothed as in many buttercups. Flowers white or red, especially on outside; the small sepals underneath petals have thick tufts of red, brown or blackish hairs, and still keep on stalk even when flowers have faded. Grows among stones, in cracks in rocks, or in grass very high up, from 2300–4270 metres. This is higher than any other flowering plant in the Alps.

Globe flower
Trollius europaeus
Height 100–700mm. Upright stem with a few branches. Leaves deeply cut into three or five strongly-toothed lobes. Those on stem are stalkless. Flowers large, 25–50mm across, with rounded, golden-yellow petals curving inwards and overlapping to make a ball, open at the top. Found in damp pastures on mountains throughout most of Europe.

Globe-headed rampion
Phyteuma orbiculare
Upright plant, 200–600mm high; unbranched. Leaves at base of stem heart-shaped, toothed, with long stalks, in a rosette. Leaves higher on stem narrow and unstalked, with rounded teeth. Flowers with narrow lobes, deep blue; many massed together in ball-shaped cluster at top of stem, 15–25mm across. Grows in poor meadows and grassy mountain slopes of central Europe.

Lichens
Many species of lichens grow on rocks of mountain-sides. A number of them form crusts on the rock surface, but some are like very small shrubs. All lichens are very slow-growing and are really two different plants growing together. One is a fungus which forms the outer layer, and in among the parts of that are cells of an alga, which is a very simple green plant.

Mosses
Mosses are small, simple, leafy plants which sometimes cover large areas of mountains. Some grow by the side of mountain streams, others grow on wet, rock ledges. They do not form seeds as flowering plants do, but make large numbers of tiny spores. These are produced in small, egg-shaped spore-cases at the end of very fine, upright stalks.

 Birds

Alpine accentor
Prunella collaris
Length 175mm. Greyish-brown upper parts. Throat white with rows of small, dark spots across it. Brown spots along sides, below wings. Thin beak. Rather shy bird, like most accentors, but common in the high mountains of central and southern Europe, above the limit of trees.

Bonelli's warbler
Phylloscopus bonelli
Length 110mm. Typically slim warbler shape; thin, pointed beak. Pale greenish-brown upper parts; white underside. Eye-stripe not very clear but yellowish rump useful for recognition. Usually well-hidden. Lives in mixed and coniferous woods in mountains, although sometimes seen lower down. Not found in Britain or far north of Europe.

Alpine chough
Pyrrhocorax graculus
Length 380mm. Medium-sized member of crow family. All black with bluish gloss, except for red legs and yellow beak. Lives high in the mountains although in winter it goes into the valleys and may be seen around villages. Searches mountain ledges for small insects, etc. in the cracks. These form main food supply and is reason for Alpine chough having slimmer beak than most other crows. Also eats berries.

Citril finch
Serinus citrinella
Length 110mm. Greenish back and grey neck; greenish-yellow underparts and rump; dark wings and tail. Typical short, thick beak of finch. Lives in mountains with coniferous woods, usually in flocks. Moves lower down in winter. Found in Alps and some mountain areas of Spain.

Redpoll
Acanthis flammea
Length 140mm. Dull brown, streaked over much of body. Black patch under beak. Red forehead. Male has pink breast in summer. Found in birch and mixed woods in mountains of south-east Europe and in far north of Europe including Britain. Often in flocks, searching in trees and bushes for seeds. Farther north its place is taken by the Arctic redpoll.

Snow finch
Montifringilla nivalis
Length 175mm. Typical finch shape. Black chin in male. White patch on wing. White outer tail feathers. Rest of body brown and grey. Bill yellow in winter, black in spring and summer. Common high up in mountains above the tree limit in summer, but comes lower in winter. Found mainly in Alps and Pyrenees. Nests in small spaces under rocks.

Grey-headed woodpecker
Picus canus
Length 250mm. May live in mountain forests but also lower down in deciduous and mixed woods and more open areas. Similar in appearance to green woodpecker, but smaller and has grey head. Male has small patch of red on top of head, but female does not. Often seen on ground looking for ants like green woodpecker does. Drums a great deal on tree trunks and branches.

Black woodpecker
Dryocopus martius
Length 450mm. Europe's largest woodpecker, but not found in Britain. Lives in forests, especially those among mountains of northern and eastern Europe. Black all over except for red top of head in male; female has smaller red patch on back of head. Nest hole in tree may be as much as 0·5 metres deep and takes two or three weeks to chip out. Eggs are laid on wood chips which may be at bottom of nest hole, but no other nesting material used.

Rock thrush
Monticola saxatilis
Length 200mm. Female mottled brown. Male has blue-grey head, back and throat; white patch on back; orange-red tail and underparts; dark wings. Found in mountainous areas of southern Europe. Shy and often hides among rocks. Migrates to Africa during winter months.

Wall creeper
Tichondroma muraria
Length 165mm. Grey back; underside black in summer, whitish in winter. Very easy to recognise by wings which have large red patches and white spots. Beak long and slightly downcurved. Not common anywhere but most likely to be seen climbing among rocks looking for insects, high up in mountains, as far as snow-line, in southern Europe. In winter, comes lower and then may be found on walls and old ruins.

Goosander
Mergus merganser
Length 625mm. A duck which dives to catch fish. Drake has body which is mainly pink underneath, dark above; glossy dark green head. Female has brown head with quite large crest; grey body and white throat. Both have long, narrow beak with small hooked end. Usually seen on lakes with woods around them, and rivers also near woods. Nests in holes either in trees or bank.

Water pipit
Anthus spinoletta spinoletta
Length 165mm. Greyish-brown upper parts; streaked underside in winter but unstreaked in summer; light eye-stripe. Sparrow-like bird with narrow beak and white outer tail

feathers. Long claws on toes. Walks rather than hops. Closely related to rock pipit and in winter both are found by shore. In spring, water pipit goes to mountains to breed. Found in central and southern Europe.

Hazel hen
Tetrastes bonasia
Length 335mm. Type of grouse found in woods and forests in mountain areas where there is thick undergrowth. Common, but becoming less so because of hunting. Brownish, speckled plumage; black throat in male, but whitish in female. Does not crouch when there is danger as do most birds of this type, but flies up. Eggs are laid near to bottom of a tree. Found mainly in central and eastern Europe, and parts of Scandinavia.

Black kite
Milvus migrans
Length 500–550mm. Dark brown plumage; forked tail which shows up well when bird is soaring. A bird of prey usually seen near lakes or rivers where it may hover over the water and catch fish in its talons. Also a scavenger and can be seen sometimes near villages. Nests in tall trees. A summer visitor to much of Europe but not Britain or Scandinavia. Winter spent in Africa.

Rough-legged buzzard
Buteo lagopus
Length 500–625mm. Mainly brown, speckled; white rump. Legs feathered right down to feet. In flight, wings are large with black patch near middle of front edge; black patch on belly; black band at end of tail. Soars over fields and moors, and hovers also. Nests in mountains of northern Europe, but winters further south.

Osprey
Pandion haliaetus
Length 525–600mm. Fish-eating bird of prey, so found only near lakes, rivers and sheltered parts of coast. Upper parts dark brown; top of head white; underparts white with pale brown band across breast. Found in northern and eastern Europe during summer. Migrates to southern Spain or Africa in winter. Flies over water about 10 metres up, then plunges down feet first to catch fish which is gripped in bird's extra-rough feet. A few ospreys nest in Scotland where they are carefully protected.

Snow bunting
Plectrophenax nivalis
Length 165mm. Male easy to recognise in summer with black and white plumage; much browner in winter. Female brown and white. Both can be identified by the large white wing patches. Common in open, rocky country even very high up in mountains. Found in more northerly parts of Europe, including Britain, and often in flocks.

Dotterel
Eudromias morinellus
Length 225mm. Brown head and back; reddish-brown underparts; white eye-stripe and throat, white breast-band. A rare bird which nests high on the mountains mainly in Scandinavia, but a few also in Scotland. Nest is a scrape on ground lined with moss. Migrates in winter to southern Italy and north Africa.

Lammergeyer
Gypaetus barbatus
Length 1–1·5 metres. Upper parts dark brown; head and underparts creamy-white and tawny; black band through eye, ending in black bristles. Long, pointed wings and wedge-shaped tail in flight. Other name is bearded vulture. Rare and found only in high mountain regions of Pyrenees. Feeds on carrion and bones which it may break by dropping from height to rocks below.

Egyptian vulture
Neophron percnopterus
Length 585–675mm. Smallest European vulture and common in mountain regions of southern Europe. Mainly white; wing-tips black; naked face; pointed head and beak rather long and narrow for a vulture. In flight, wings show bold black and white pattern. Scavenger. Soars on air currents and when food is spotted will drop down at once and this will attract any other nearby vultures.

Ptarmigan
Lagopus mutus
Length 350mm. Plump and rather chicken-like bird. Well-camouflaged whatever the time of year. In summer and autumn upper parts are brown, mottled with black; underparts and wings are white. In winter, whole bird looks white. At all times male has black stripe through eye and red eyebrows. Lives in mountain areas of Scotland and Scandinavia, higher up than the tree limit.

Peregrine falcon
Falco peregrinus
Length 400–500mm. Bird of prey once common all over Europe, but now much rarer because of shooting and also the effects in its body of poisonous chemicals sprayed on farm crops and eaten by its prey. Male blue-grey upper parts; lighter and barred underneath. Female browner. Can dive at very great speed with wings partly folded when catching birds or small mammals. Used to be trained by falconers and used for hunting. Male called a *tiercel.*

 # Mammals

Alpine marmot
Marmota marmota
Body length 575mm, tail 160mm. Found in open country in mountains, between 1000–3000 metres. Large, rather plump rodent with rounded head, short ears and short tail. Marmots are alert animals, sitting upright on hind legs to keep watch. They live in colonies and make burrows down which they dash at the slightest hint of danger. They hibernate during winter months. Mainly in Alps, but introduced into Pyrenees and Carpathians.

Spanish lynx
Lynx pardina
Body length 850mm–1·1 metres, tail 120–130mm. Very rare animal indeed, found only in Spain, in Doñana reserve and possibly still in the mountains. Smaller than European lynx. Yellowish-brown; heavily spotted; cheek ruffs; black ear tufts and tip of tail. Feeds on birds and small mammals, especially rabbits, but will sometimes tackle a deer.

European lynx
Lynx lynx
Body length 800mm–1·3 metres, tail 110–240mm. Large cat-like animal with long legs. Tawny colour, slightly spotted mainly on legs. Short tail with black tip. Ruff of longer hairs around cheeks and tufts on ears. Europe's largest cat, fairly widespread in lonely mountain areas of northern, eastern and central Europe, but not common. Active mainly at dusk.

Ibex
Capra ibex
Body length 1·25–1·5 metres, tail 120–150mm. The ibex is the true wild goat—not just a domestic goat gone back to wild state. Lives in high mountains of Alps and Pyrenees between 2000–3500 metres. Feeds on shrubs and grasses. Grey with black markings; beard; large, backward-curving horns larger in males than females. Very sure-footed. Males found on higher ground than females.

Chamois
Rupicapra rupicapra
Body length 1·1–1·3 metres, tail 30–40mm. Looks very much like a brown goat with dark stripes along light-coloured face. Horns small and slender, curved back at ends. Lives in high forests and above, right up to snow-line. Comes lower down mountains in winter. Very sure-footed. Females and young move in herds.

Brown bear
Ursus arctos
Body length 1·5–2·5 metres, tail 60–140mm. Now found only in forests in mountains of northern Scandinavia, Pyenees and eastern Europe. Not likely to be mistaken for any other animal. Feeds on almost anything including fruit, insects, fish, carrion and honey. Rests in underground den during winter. Young stay with mother for a long time.

 # Fish

Lake trout
Salmo trutta
Length 200–500mm. Greenish-brown above, silvery underneath; dull red spots on sides. Lake trout is a form of brown trout. Lives in large, cold, mountain and northern lakes. In autumn, adults move into streams to breed. Young spend several years in streams before swimming to lakes. Feed on many kinds of water animals.

Char
Salvelinus alpinus
Length 450mm. A member of the salmon family, very similar in appearance to trout. Lives in deep mountain lakes.

Whitefish
Species of *Coregonus*
Not really a single species at all, but a group name for a number of similar species. Related to salmon and trout, but silvery-white all over which is reason for name. Live in mountain lakes and rivers.

Grayling
Thymållus thymallus
Length 350mm. Common in cold mountain rivers. Flesh has a smell like that of thyme. Member of salmon family. Very similar in appearance to trout; greenish back; silver or yellow sides with small, dark spots along them.

Trees & Shrubs

Norway spruce
Ht up to 40m
(p12)

Silver fir
Ht up to 50m
(p183)

Scots pine
Ht up to 30m
(p151)

Larch
Ht up to 50m
(p12)

Alpine rhododendron
Ht up to 1m
(p183)

Mountain pine
Ht up to 3·5m
(p183)

Mezereon
Ht 0·5 – 1m
(p183)

Dwarf juniper
Ht 100 – 150mm
(p183)

Bilberry
Ht up to 0.5m
(p151)

Alpine rose
Ht 0.5 – 2m
(p183)

Herbs

Gentian
Ht 50 – 100mm
(p183)

Wild pink
Ht up to 400mm
(p184)

Yellow wolf's bane
Ht 0·5 – 1m
(p184)

Fragrant orchid
Ht 150 – 400mm
(p184)

Alpine trefoil
Ht 50 – 200mm
(p184)

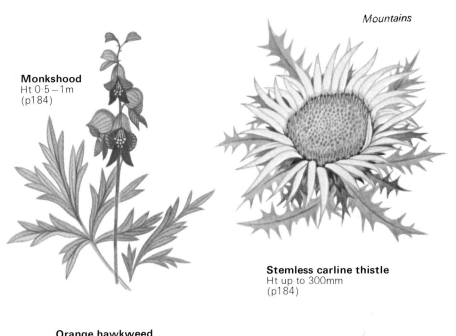

Monkshood
Ht 0·5 – 1m
(p184)

Stemless carline thistle
Ht up to 300mm
(p184)

Orange hawkweed
Ht 200 – 500mm
(p184)

Edelweiss
Ht 50 – 200mm
(p185)

Musky saxifrage
Ht 25 – 75mm
(p185)

Spring anemone
Ht 50 – 150mm
(p185)

Spiked bell-flower
Ht 200mm – 1m
(p185)

Moss campion
Ht 50mm
(p185)

Mountain buttercup
Ht 160 – 300mm
(p185)

Globe flower
Ht 100 – 700mm
(p186)

Ice crowfoot
Low-growing
(p185)

Globe-headed rampion
Ht 200 – 600mm
(p186)

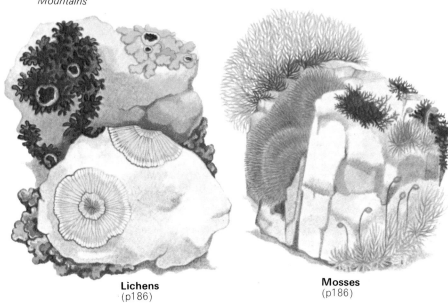

Lichens
(p186)

Mosses
(p186)

Birds

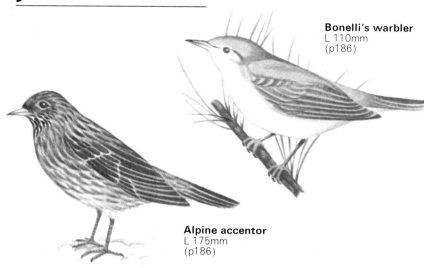

Bonelli's warbler
L 110mm
(p186)

Alpine accentor
L 175mm
(p186)

Alpine chough
L 380mm
(p186)

Redpoll
L 140mm
(p187)

Snow finch
L 175mm
(p187)

Citril finch
L 110mm
(p186)

199

Grey-headed woodpecker
L 250mm
(p187)

Black woodpecker
L 450mm
(p187)

Green woodpecker
L 300mm
(p17)

Crossbill
L 140mm
(p18)

Crossbill

female

male

Greater spotted woodpecker
L 230mm
(p17)

Wall creeper
L 165mm
(p187)

Rock thrush
L 200mm
(p187)

Dipper
L 180mm
(p88)

Grey Heron
L 1m
(p87)

Water pipit
L 165mm
(p187)

Goosander
L 625mm
(p187)

Raven
L 630mm
(p156)

Hazel hen
L 335mm
(p188)

Black kite
L 500 – 550mm
(p188)

Rough-legged buzzard
L 500—625mm
(p188)

Osprey
L 525—600mm
(p188)

Snow bunting
L 165mm
(p188)

Dotterel
L 225mm
(p188)

Lammergeyer
L 1 – 1·5m
(p188)

Egyptian vulture
L 585 – 675mm
(p189)

Golden eagle
L (f) 910mm
(p154)

Ptarmigan
L 350mm
(p189)

Peregrine falcon
L 400–500mm
(p189)

Mammals

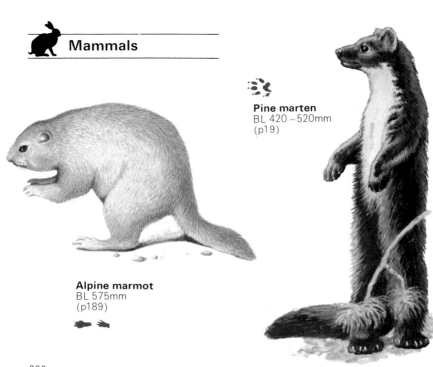

Pine marten
BL 420–520mm
(p19)

Alpine marmot
BL 575mm
(p189)

Mountain hare
BL 570 – 610mm
(p156)

Spanish lynx
BL 850mm – 1·1m
(p189)

European lynx
BL 800mm – 1·3m
(p189)

Chamois
BL 1·1–1·3m
(p190)

Ibex
BL 1·25–1·5m
(p189)

Brown bear
BL 1·5–2·5m·
(p190)

Fish

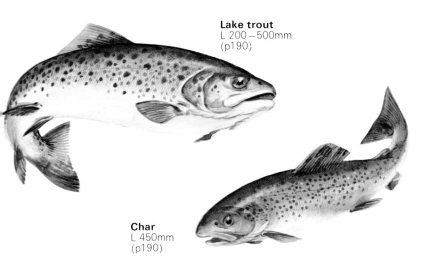

Lake trout
L 200 – 500mm
(p190)

Char
L 450mm
(p190)

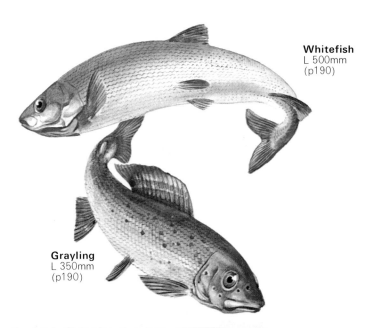

Whitefish
L 500mm
(p190)

Grayling
L 350mm
(p190)

Cities & Parks

Cities hardly seem to be the kind of place where much wildlife is likely to be found, but it is surprising just what will live in them. Plants need soil, sunlight, air and moisture. Animals need a supply of food and a place where they can breed without being disturbed. All these requirements can be found in parts of cities and so it is not all that surprising that some animals and plants are quite able to adapt to living in these places.

Consider the buildings. There are office blocks and similar places where plenty of people move around during the day, but where there is silence at night. These buildings are often tall and have numbers of small ledges, so that in many ways they resemble cliff faces.

In the commercial parts of a city, especially near a river, there are warehouses which offer large spaces;

Don't forget built-up areas in your search for wildlife.

they often contain plenty of boxes and suchlike for hiding places, and many of them remain undisturbed for long periods.

There are always plenty of hotels, restaurants and cafes in cities. These might be thought to have little to attract wildlife because people are around for much of the day and night, but at the back are the dustbins where unwanted food is thrown. Unwanted by people perhaps, but a food supply for a number of animals.

Houses, too, are to be found in cities, many with tiny gardens that provide footholds for plants; these homes often hold willing feeders for the birds.

Many cities have rivers running through them. Such rivers are usually badly polluted, although this is not always the case. London's famous river, the Thames, used to be so polluted that little could live in its lower reaches. But now it is getting cleaner, with fewer harmful materials being poured into it and a number of species of fish are beginning to find their way back.

Railways and roads cut channels through the cities, and sometimes prove to be unexpected haunts of wildlife; plants especially thrive among the edges of the track ballast of railway cuttings.

Any building site left unworked for a time will soon become covered with seedlings – and a feeding area for birds. In most cities there are a few such places where buildings

Parks are convenient places for naturalists.

have been knocked down and for some reason left unused. It is always well worth investigating those areas.

But possibly the most interesting places in any city are the parks, because here gardeners have planted foreign species to share the park with the native plants that can survive there. There is usually a pond or lake which will attract water birds, and the open space with plenty of trees is ideal for perching birds.

On the outskirts of the city are the suburbs. Thousands and thousands of houses, each with a garden, large or small. The total area of all these gardens makes the suburbs very large nature reserves. Many animals and plants have found suburban gardens just as good as the country for living in. There is food in the form of leaves and fruit, and meat, along with all sorts of other tit-bits that are put out by the people there. There are breeding-places and hiding-places too. But there *are* predators, in the shape of cats and dogs.

Life in Cities & Parks

Although there is plenty of wildlife in cities, it is sometimes difficult to study it there. A city is not a small habitat like a pond, nor can it be divided into zones as can the sea-shore, but if you just keep your eyes open a city will show very well just how living things make the most of their opportunities and adapt themselves to slightly different surroundings.

Birds, for example, must have nesting sites and a city will provide plenty of these, although some would appear to be rather strange. It has been known for a pigeon to nest on top of a bus stop, and a sparrow to build one among the ornamental ironwork of a large gate outside Buckingham Palace! Birds that prefer to nest in trees and bushes usually have little difficulty in finding something to suit them thanks to the parks that can be found in most cities, where there are plenty of trees.

Buildings have many ledges, drain-pipes, chimney pots, holes and cracks that make good substitutes for the cliff ledges or hollow trees that city birds might have chosen had they lived in the country. It was the tremendous number of possible places for nest-building that brought increasing numbers of black red-starts to London in the 1940s, a time when there were many buildings left partly knocked down and empty after being bombed during air-raids.

Cities are warm places and the temperature is always a few degrees higher in the centre of one than in the surrounding countryside. All the large buildings such as hotels, banks and office-blocks are heated during the winter and there are gratings and ducts out of which warm air flows. This extra warmth in cities is another attraction to wildlife, especially birds when they want to roost at night.

Several years ago, it was noticed that large flocks of starlings were flying into London at dusk from the suburbs. They were coming to roost, settling in huge numbers on build-ings and trees where, even if the lights were bright, it was warm. They still do this and each starling has its own roosting place and should it die, several days will go by before its space is filled by another starling.

Animals will not live in any place unless there is food for them. In cities there is often plenty and, once again, it is birds which seem to have benefited most. Thousands of tour-ists and workers in cities eat sand-wiches which they bring for their lunch. For much of the year they eat them outside and crumbs are bound to be dropped which will bring a sparrow or pigeon to feed on them. Very few people can then resist

deliberately giving more of their sandwiches to the birds; this attracts still more and it is a common sight in almost any city to see small birds hopping around people's feet for this kind of food.

In earlier years when traffic was horse-drawn, sparrows obtained much of their food from the oats that were scattered on the roads from horses' nosebags. Now that this food supply has gone, most cities have fewer sparrows than they did in the past, although that is sometimes hard to believe.

Today sparrows often have to face another problem for they have become prey for kestrels. In the country, kestrels feed largely on small mammals such as voles, and they can often be seen hovering over fields while their keen eyes search for the slightest sign of a meal. In cities, however, they tend to catch the small birds that are easier to see, especially in the parks. Their eggs are laid on ledges of buildings and during the breeding season they can sometimes be heard making their strange mewing calls that mingle with the noise of traffic.

Parks may often provide a certain amount of protection for wildlife. For example, in the country rabbits may well be a nuisance and therefore farmers may shoot them, but should there be a few living in a park they are much more likely to

Cities provide a variety of habitats for birds.

become pleasant attractions. Here they will be looked after rather than killed.

It is not often that wild mammals are actually seen in cities. Occasionally a rat or a mouse may be spotted around the warehouses down by a river. But seen or not, they are there, often causing a lot of damage.

Most mammals, of course, prefer to move about at night, which makes it difficult to gather information about them in cities. Foxes are now commonly seen in suburbs and it is quite possible that they will soon venture further in, to scavenge from the waste bins at the back of cafes and restaurants. In fact, some people believe that they are already doing this. Foxes and some birds are therefore changing their normal habits in order to be able to make use of what the city has to offer.

Cats and dogs are city mammals also. Many cats have become quite capable of looking after themselves so that they are almost wild. Dogs on the whole are still kept by people and for anyone interested in the various breeds, city parks are excellent places for observing them.

Parks are interesting in other ways, too. They are, of course, open spaces that are like country fields in many ways, but they have an additional advantage. Because most of them have flower beds and special trees planted, it is possible to see species of plants which it might not be otherwise possible to see without a great deal of travelling.

Many parks have lakes, large or small, that will attract birds and a few even have collections of waterfowl on them. In London, the lake in St James's Park has a fine collection that was started by King Charles II in the 17th century and it is possible to see pelicans, cormorants, and many species of ducks, as well as coots and moorhens.

If you are interested in wild flowers it is worth looking out for patches of waste land in cities and towns. Here you will find thistles, bindweeds and other small flowering plants, as well as shrubs such as the buddleia. The purple heads of blossom of the buddleia attract so many butterflies in the summer that it is often known as the butterfly bush. It can be found growing in the most unlikely places, such as in the cracked brickwork of a building.

In warmer countries like those around the Mediterranean, cities offer a variety of plants, from palm trees to the beautiful bougainvilleas that make almost every Mediterranean town so colourful.

Look out for wild flowers in waste land.

Things to look for in Cities & Parks

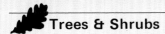

Trees & Shrubs

Lime
Tilia europaea
Height up to 25 metres. Bark smooth, grey. Leaves heart-shaped, toothed, fairly soft, light green, 60–100mm long and with a long stalk. Tree can be recognised in winter by buds which have only two scales covering them, one much larger than the other. Flowers hang in bunches of four to ten on long stalks with a long, strap-like *bract* attached; creamy-white, sweet-smelling. Fruit ball-shaped, hard, grey. Also called linden.

Plane
Platanus acerifolia
Height up to 35 metres. Bark greyish-green, but peels off in large flakes. New bark underneath is creamy-yellow so trunk has patchy appearance, and it is easy to recognise. Leaves large, with several pointed lobes. Separate male and female flowers in ball-shaped clusters on hanging stalks. Balls of seeds formed after pollination break up and scatter during winter. Often called London plane because so many are planted there, but also found in France, Spain and Italy.

Maidenhair
Ginkgo biloba
Height up to 30 metres, more or less pyramid shaped. Bark rough, brown. Leaves in bunches, growing from short shoot; fan-shaped with notch in centre of outer edge dividing leaf into two lobes. Introduced into Europe from Japan in 1730, but most likely first grown in China. Sometimes called a 'living fossil' because fossils show that forms of maidenhair trees existed millions of years ago.

Horse chestnut
Aesculus hippocastanum
Height up to 25 metres. In winter, large buds covered by brown, sticky scales. Beneath each one is a horse-shoe-shaped scar with raised dots in it showing position of previous year's leaf. Leaves made up of five or seven large leaflets attached to central stalk making them look like fingers of a hand. Flowers white, sometimes pink, in large upright masses. Fruit with large, glossy, brown seeds ('conkers') inside spiky, green husk.

Locust
Robinia pseudoacacia
Height up to 27 metres. Bark pale grey and patterned with thick ridges. Leaves long, up to 300mm, made up of many oval leaflets on either side of stalk. Two small spines on twig at base of each leaf. Flowers white, shaped like pea flowers, in hanging chains. Seeds in greyish, flat pods. Introduced from America where early settlers used wood for fencing, handles for tools and shafts of carts.

Laburnum
Laburnum anagyroides
Small tree, up to 7 metres. Bark smooth, dark olive green or brown. Leaves with three leaflets on long stalk. Flowers golden-yellow, shaped like pea flowers, in long hanging chains. Seeds poisonous, in dark brown pods which stay on tree during winter even when empty. Also called golden rain. Wood in centre of trunk and branches is very dark brown and is used for wood carving and musical instruments.

Holly
Ilex aquifolium
Height 5–8 metres. Leaves dark green, glossy, with wavy edges

having sharp spines. Some garden varieties have creamy-yellow markings around edges. Flowers small, white or green. Male and female flowers usually on separate trees. Females produce clusters of bright red berries. Holly twigs with berries are very popular as Christmas decoration. Grows wild over much of Europe. In parks, may be grown as tree or used for hedges.

Cedar
Cedrus libani
Height up to 30 metres. Cedar of Lebanon is a very impressive tree with widely-spreading branches. Conifer. Bark grey, smooth when young but with many splits when older. Leaves short, narrow needles, in bluish-green bunches of twenty or more on short side shoots. Cones upright, barrel-shaped, green at first but becoming brown when ripe after about two years. Grows wild in mountains of Lebanon and Turkey but single trees sometimes grown in European parks.

Tree of Heaven
Ailanthus altissima
Height up to 28 metres. Bark black with network of paler cracks. Leaves large, often over 300mm long, made up of thirteen to twenty-five oval, pointed leaflets not opposite one another. When young, leaves have bronze tint. In winter, twigs show small, rounded buds with large leaf scar under each. Flowers greenish and not often noticed. Seeds have twisted, papery wing. Native to China and introduced into Europe in 1751. Grows well in cities because it can stand smoke.

Date palm
Phoenix dactylifera
Height 4·5 metres or more. Trunk very ridged and rough with remains of old leaf stalks sticking out. Leaves very long, up to 2 metres, made up of large number of long narrow, pointed leaflets. Leaves spread out 3 metres or more and give top of tree a feathery appearance from a distance. Separate male and female flowers. Fruit, if formed, is well-known, sticky date with hard stone inside. Native to north Africa but grown in other hot, dry, European countries. Many species of palms likely to be seen in Mediterranean towns.

Ornamental cherry
Species of *Prunus*
Many different varieties. Often called Japanese cherries and given Japanese names. Most are small trees but some grow up to 7 metres or more. Bark brown, sometimes shiny, with raised bands like scars running across the trunk. Leaves more or less oval with toothed edges and slender point, mid-green and turning yellow, orange and deep red in autumn. Flowers single or double, 30—50mm across, hanging in dense clusters, white or pink. Grown in parks and along roadside, especially in suburbs.

Ornamental almond
Prunus amygdalus
Height 6—8 metres. Small tree planted in parks and alongside roads for beauty of its blossom, which appears in February or March, before leaves show. Flowers 30—50mm across, five pink petals. Leaves oval, long and pointed with toothed edges. Fruit oval with green, rough, tough outer skin. Stone inside is hard, woody, pale brown and pitted with small holes. Seed in it has brown coat, white inside and has pleasant taste. Introduced from western Asia.

Mimosa
Acacia dealbata
Height up to 7 metres, sometimes more. Leaves grey-green with many

small leaflets so that they look almost like fern fronds; covered with fine, silvery hairs when young. Flowers very sweet-smelling, golden yellow and ball-shaped, hanging down in clusters. Mainly seen in Mediterranean countries, especially French Riviera, but occasionally in other countries where winters are mild. Also called silver wattle.

Magnolia
Species of *Magnolia*
Small tree or shrub with spreading branches. Height 3—4 metres. Leaves mid-green, long-oval. Flowers large, 125—150mm across, shaped like large tulips with small number of large petals, white inside and rosy-purple on outside. Flowers open before leaves unfold. Several species, all very beautiful. Some are native to China and Far East, others to north and central America.

Rhododendron
Species of *Rhododendron*
A group of plants containing many species from small shrubs to trees up to 18 metres high. Most of those in parks are shrubs about 2—3 metres high. Leaves long, glossy, dark green, oval with blunt tips. Flowers in clusters, funnel-shaped. Large variety of colours including white, pink, orange, yellow, red and purple, or a mixture of these. Rhododendrons come mainly from Asia, including the Himalayas, although a few are from America and Europe.

Bougainvillea
Bougainvillea glabra
Climbing shrub, up to 6 metres. Oval leaves, tapering to point. Flowers small, white or yellow, in threes, surrounded by large, showy, triangular *bracts* which are various shades of red or purple. These dry up later and act as parachutes for seeds. Common in Mediterranean

countries. Named after Louis Antoine de Bougainville who made a voyage around the world in 1766—69.

Azalea
Species of *Rhododendron*
Shrubs, usually no more than about 2 metres high, often much less. Many species. Leaves rounded or oval. Flowers trumpet shaped but ends of petals may be pointed. Colours vary but usually bright. White, yellow, orange; purple common. Once thought to be a different group from rhododendrons but now included with them. Will not grow on lime or chalk. Some native to Far East, others to north America.

Buddleia
Buddleia davidii
Height 1—5 metres. Strong-growing and wide-spreading shrub. Leaves 100—250mm long, toothed, dark green above and whitish underneath. Flowers small and tube-like, but massed in purplish clusters, up to 300mm long at end of arching stems. Grown in parks, but also wild on waste ground, beside railway lines and even in cracks in buildings. Attracts numbers of butterflies when in flower. Native to China.

Box
Buxus sempervirens
Height up to 6 metres. Slow-growing evergreen. Leaves oval with smooth edges, glossy on upper surface and grow opposite one another on stem. Grows wild, but often seen in parks where it is used for hedges and also clipped into shape of animals. This is known as the art of *topiary*. Wood is hard and used for mallets and rulers.

Camellia
Species of *Camellia*
Shrub. Height up to 2·5 metres. Leaves glossy, deep green, oval with pointed tips. Flowers 50—75mm

across, open bowl-shaped, colours vary but are white, red, or shades of pink. Several species and many different varieties grown in parks and gardens. May be grown in tubs, flower beds or against walls. Native to India, China and Japan.

Rose
Species of *Rosa*
Shrub up to 1·5 metres. Very popular and common in flower beds in parks. Stems prickly. Leaves dark green, often glossy, made up of several toothed leaflets. Flowers in a very large variety of colours, 100–140mm across, many petals rolled over at the edge. Those most likely to be seen are hybrid tea roses, but floribunda roses are becoming very popular. These have more open flowers with fewer petals.

 Herbs

Oxford ragwort
Senecio squalidus
Height 200–300mm. Branched. Almost hairless. Leaves lobed, each may be toothed and end lobe has sharp point. Many flower-heads, 150–200mm across, outer flowers yellow, like strap-shaped petals, usually thirteen inner flowers packed into raised mound. Green bracts under heads have black tips. Grows on old walls and waste ground. Introduced from southern Italy where it grows on volcanic rock.

Hedge bindweed
Calystegia sepium
Creeping and climbing plant, up to 3 metres. Smooth, twining stem. Leaves arrow-shaped, up to 150mm long. Flowers grow singly, large, trumpet-shaped, white or pink. Close up at night. Found on waste ground where it may climb up and cover wire-netting fences, etc.

Field bindweed
Convolvulus arvensis
Creeping and climbing plant up to 750mm long, often climbing up other plants. Leaves heart- or arrow-shaped, 20–50mm long. Flowers about 30mm across, white or pink, scented and visited by many insects. Very common on waste ground and beside roads and railways.

Tea-plant
Lycium halimifolium
Shrub with greyish-white stems that arch over, up to 2·5 metres long. Leaves narrow-oval and bluntly pointed, greyish-green, up to 60mm long. Flowers singly or in small clusters, each with five rosy-purple petals which later turn pale brown. Fruit scarlet, fleshy, long-oval, 10–20mm. Full name is Duke of Argyll's tea-plant, probably introduced from south-east Europe or Asia, and grows on walls and waste ground.

Wall rocket
Diplotaxis muralis
Stem upright, branched from the bottom, 150–600mm high, with few leaves. Most leaves form rosette on ground; up to 100mm long, lobed, and narrowing into long stalk. Flowers lemon-yellow, about 100mm across, four petals. Seed-pods long and very narrow, held upright at an angle to stem. Grows on walls and waste ground, sometimes by railways.

Common mallow
Malva sylvestris
Height 450–900mm. Stem slightly hairy and usually upright, but sometimes partly lying down. Leaves near base are roundish with few blunt lobes. Stem leaves with five to seven triangular lobes, sometimes with dark spot. Flowers 25–40mm across, in clusters between stem and leaf-stalk. Each has five reddish-purple petals

with darker stripes, deep notch in end, not joined together. Fruit a flat, round nutlet. Common on waste ground.

White dead-nettle
Lamium album
Height 200–600mm. Creeping underground stems and upright flowering stems. Leaves heart-shaped, toothed edges, 30–70mm long, in pairs, opposite one another. Flowers in clusters between stem and leaves, each 20–25mm long, tube with hood and lower lip, white. Visited by bumble bees. Very common in waste places.

Spear thistle
Cirsium vulgare
Height 300mm–1·5 metres. Stem upright, grooved and partly with spiny wings. Branches near top. Stem leaves without stalk, wavy, lobed, very prickly edges; long, narrow, pointed lobe at end; prickly hairs on upper surface, rough underneath. Flower-heads pale reddish-purple, 15–25mm across, brush-like with ball-shaped mass of spiny bracts around lower part of flowers. Visited by many insects such as bees and butterflies. Seeds with long hairs to help float through air. Found in gardens and waste places.

Wall barley
Hordeum murinum
Height 60–600mm. Stem smooth, partly covered by ends of leaves which wrap around it. Leaves long, narrow and pointed, 20–200mm, rough to touch. Flowers in dense mass, 40–120mm high and 10–30mm wide at end of stem. Each flower has long, bristly hairs called *awns* which spread out slightly. Flowers between May and August. Wall barley is a very common grass on waste ground, especially near bottom of buildings and walls.

Stinging nettle
Urtica dioica
Height 300mm–1·5 metres. Spreads by means of creeping underground stems which send up new shoots in spring. Stem with coarse hairs. Leaves 40–80mm long, heart-shaped but not very wide, pointed tip, covered with stinging hairs, edges with large teeth. Flowers small, green, in hanging, long, narrow catkins. Very common on waste ground where there is plenty of rubble. Flowers between June and November in patches.

Toadflax
Linaria vulgaris
Height 300–800mm. Upright stem with branches on upper part. Many leaves, narrow, pointed, smooth edges, 30–80mm long. Flowers yellow with upper and lower lips at end of tube, and long spur at back which may be up to 30mm long; lower lip has orange spot. About twenty flowers near top of stem. Usually many plants together since they spread by underground stems. Found in waste places, hedgerows and fields; flowers between June and October.

Rosebay willow-herb
Chamaenerion angustifolium
Also called fireweed. Height 300mm–1·2 metres. Stem upright, often reddish near top. Many leaves, 50–150mm long, narrow each end and with long, pointed tip; some plants have leaves with toothed edges, others with smooth. Many flowers on upper part of stem; 20–30mm across, bright reddish-purple, four notched petals, upper pair slightly different size from lower; four purple sepals show between petals. Seed pod long and narrow with four angles. Seeds with tufts of white hairs to help drift through air. Grows in gardens and building sites, often in large patches.

Tulip
Species of *Tulipa*
About 100 different species. Planted in flower-beds in gardens and parks to flower during March, April and May. Height up to 600mm. Grows from bulb. Most leaves near base of stem, large, oval but many have edges rolled over or wavy; deep green, smooth waxy surface. Usually single flower on end of smooth, upright stem; vase-shaped, six petals which may be rounded or pointed; great variety of colours. Introduced into Europe from Turkey over 300 years ago.

Daffodil
Species of *Narcissus*
About sixty species but around 8000 cultivated varieties. Probably the most popular of spring flowers. Grown from bulbs and planted in gardens and parks. Leaves long, narrow, strap-like, greyish-green. Daffodil has single flower at end of smooth, upright, leafless stem. Other types of *Narcissus* may have several flowers. Petals usually yellow or orange, in form of trumpet, either long or very short. Six sepals, very much like petals, usually white or yellow, spread out behind trumpet. Native species of daffodil grow over much of central and southern Europe.

Crocus
Species of *Crocus*
More than seventy species. Those in parks usually flowering during February and March, but others flower earlier. Leaves stiff, narrow, deep green with whitish stripe up centre. Flower vase-shaped, 100mm high, six more or less oval petals, usually white, golden yellow, or shades of purple. Most wild crocuses are found on fairly high ground in countries to the north and east of the Mediterranean.

 # Birds

Pigeon
Columba livia
Length 325mm. Colour of feathers varies; may be bluish-grey or reddish-brown with patches of black and white, black bars on wings. Grey birds have green and purple sheen on neck feathers. Very common in towns and cities where they may be a nuisance. City pigeons are descended from those that were kept for food during the Middle Ages, which in turn were descended from wild rock-doves.

Kestrel
Falco tinnunculus
Length 338mm. Bird of prey. Brown back; male has grey head and tail, but female has brown upper parts. Both have speckled underparts. When seen hovering, note pointed wings and black bar near end of tail. Feeds on mice and voles in country but probably takes more sparrows in cities.

Collared dove
Streptopelia decaocto
Length 315mm. Greyish-brown upper parts, grey below. Small head, black and white collar around back of neck. In flight shows white tip to tail and dark ends to wings. Once only found in Balkans, but since 1930s has spread rapidly across Europe. Now seen in parks and gardens, sometimes feeding with other pigeons.

Robin
Erithacus rubecula
Length 140mm. Olive-brown above; orange-red breast, throat and forehead; white belly. Seen in parks and gardens in Britain where it is very bold. In most of Europe, robin is very shy and keeps to woods. Feeds on insects, seeds and worms. Sings well

and this is way it stakes out territory. Young robins have no red colour; breast is creamy brown and speckled.

Magpie
Pica pica
Length 450mm (half of this is tail). Very clear black and white pattern and long tail make this bird easy to recognise when perched and flying. Large strong beak. Common in parks but very wary of people. Often in pairs and can be heard chattering. They hoard food they do not need and may also take shiny objects. This has given rise to the idea that magpies are thieves and will take jewellery.

Bluetit
Parus caeruleus
Length 112mm. Small, active bird. Top of head, wings and tail blue; white cheeks; black streaks on neck, face and throat; yellow underparts; back green. Very popular bird, common in parks and gardens. Able to learn quickly, for example has learnt how to get at cream in milk-bottles on suburban doorsteps by pecking through metal tops. Does not often feed on ground.

Wren
Troglodytes troglodytes
Length 100mm. Very small, brownish bird, with small tail barred with dark brown, often cocked upwards. Grey eye-stripe. Thin, pointed beak. Very restless, hopping about in undergrowth after small insects and spiders. Very loud song for such a small bird. May sometimes be seen in parks and gardens. Many die in hard winters.

House sparrow
Passer domesticus
Length 145mm. Rather drab brown and grey bird. Male has grey crown and black bib. Female much plainer. Thick beak and short legs. Large numbers seen everywhere in cities, feeding on ground. In spring, males display by chirping with head well up, tail up and wings pointing downwards.

Starling
Sturnus vulgaris
Length 215mm. Black but with purple and green sheen in sunlight, speckled with white or cream in winter. Fairly long, narrow beak and short tail. Walks jerkily. Very noisy and quarrelsome when feeding in group. Very common in towns and cities. May be seen flying in flocks of thousands.

Pied wagtail
Motacilla alba
Length 175mm. Black and white with long tail that is jerked up and down as bird walks. Female has grey back. Narrow, pointed beak. In flight white feathers on outer edges of tail can be seen. Often alone, or in small groups. Fairly common in towns, often near water. May roost in large flocks.

Blackbird
Turdus merula
Length 250mm. Male all black with yellow beak. Female brown, lighter underneath and slightly speckled; brown beak. Usually seen in ones and twos, in parks and gardens, often scratching around under shrubs for insects and worms. Very sweet song and is main singer in dawn chorus.

Wood pigeon
Columba palumbus
Length 400mm. Grey head, neck, back and tail. Breast pale purple-grey. White patch on side of neck as well as purple and green. White wing bar. Largest European pigeon. Used to be found only in country, but now common in cities, often with other pigeons, feeding on ground in parks. Will become very tame. Disliked by farmers because it damages crops.

Black redstart
Phoenicurus ochruros
Length 140mm. Male mainly black or dark grey, female grey-brown; both have reddish rump and tail. Narrow pointed beak. Often sings from ledges on high buildings. Has only nested in Britain within last fifty years; now builds nests in cracks in old buildings. Northern birds migrate in winter to Mediterranean and southern Asia. Feeds mostly on insects which it catches while flying.

Black-headed gull
Larus ridibundus
Length 375mm. Grey back, black tips to wings, rest of body white except for head which becomes dark brown in spring and summer. This is lost in winter and head is white with small dark ear patch. Red legs and beak. Has become town bird within last seventy years. Breeds mostly in marshy places, often a long way inland. A scavenger in town, eating scraps, but away from town feeds on crabs, worms, snails and insects. Call is very harsh.

Pintail
Anas acuta
Length 700mm. Attractive duck sometimes seen on park lakes, usually in pairs. Male has brown head, white throat; rest of body grey with some darker, drooping wing feathers. Neck quite long. Male can be recognised by long, spiky tail, held well up. Female mottled brown all over and has fairly pointed tail.

Pochard
Aythya ferina
Length 450mm. Small groups often on park lakes with tufted ducks. Male has reddish-brown head, black breast and grey back. Female all brown. Diving duck feeding mainly on roots, leaves, buds and small water animals.

Tufted duck
Aythya fuligula
Length 425mm. Very common diving duck on fresh-water. Male easily recognised by white sides which show up clearly against rest of dark body; long, drooping tuft of feathers down back of head and neck. Yellow eyes. Female brown with much smaller tuft.

Pelican
Pelecanus onocrotalus
Length over 1·5 metres. Only likely to be seen on very large lakes where there are ornamental birds. Not likely to be mistaken for anything else. Mainly white; *very* large beak, hooked at tip and with pouch underneath for scooping up fish.

Mandarin duck
Aix galericulata
Length 450mm. Very striking and attractive duck, on park lakes. Male easily recognised by orange-brown wing fan. Female grey-brown and less attractive. First bred in China.

 # Mammals

Pipistrelle
Pipistrellus pipistrellus
Body length 33–52mm. The smallest European bat, commonly seen near buildings in the evening, flying quickly but with much twisting and changing direction. Mouse-like body, but with very blunt face; large ears although not as large as some species. Greyish-brown fur; wing membranes dark grey, stretched between front and back legs, and between back legs and tail. Feeds on insects caught while flying.

House mouse
Mus musculus
Body length 75–103mm. Small mouse with tail as long as body.

Pointed muzzle. Usually grey all over, but some kinds may live partly in buildings and partly in fields and these may be browner with white underneath. Moves about at night and so not often seen. Can climb and swim. House mice live in large family groups and in places such as warehouses there may be very large numbers.

Brown rat
Rattus norvegicus
Body length 214—273mm. Mouse-shaped but much larger. Although called brown rat, the rather shaggy fur is greyish-brown and can even be black on upperparts, whitish below. Rather shy, active mainly at night. Lives in warehouses, cellars, sewers, etc., and will eat almost anything. Rats breed all the year round and have three to five litters a year with about seven in each. Many of the young die, but huge numbers of rats exist in every town and city.

Fox terrier
Small, lively dog with short, up-right tail. Alert expression. Small, V-shaped ears which drop forward. There are smooth-haired and wire-haired breeds. Both about 300mm high. Colour mainly white with black or brown patches.

Labrador retriever
Large, very strong, good-tempered dog. Ears hang down. Tail fairly long. Broad head and deep chest. Coat short, usually black or yellowish-brown. Height 550mm or more. Used as guide dogs for the blind.

Poodle
Lively, alert, intelligent dog with small feet and a dainty walk. Rather long head and fairly long ears that hang. Coat slightly wavy or curly and usually trimmed in some special way. Colour white, black or brown. Height from 270mm upwards.

Spaniel
Cocker spaniel medium-sized, sleek coat with some long hair, especially around feet. Very long, hanging ears. Short tail, rather large feet. Springer spaniel much heavier dog with deep body and fairly short legs. Colours usually black, brown, or brown and white. Height about 500mm for springer, less for cocker. Used to flush game in shooting.

Dachshund
Small, long-bodied dog with very short legs. Long tail and longish head. Coat may be smooth or long-haired. Height less than 250mm. Colour black or brown.

Corgi
Small, low, quite heavy-looking dog but lively. Short or medium-length hair. Pointed ears held upright. Rather foxy face with alert expression. Short tail or tail-less. Height 300mm or less Colour often golden-brown with white chest.

Alsatian
Large, powerful, wolf-like dog, with deep chest, long legs and long tail. Pointed muzzle, alert expression. V-shaped ears held upright and pointing slightly forward. Colour usually black and grey. Short, rather coarse hair. Height over 600mm. Often used as guard and police dogs.

Invertebrates

Two-spot ladybird
Adalia bipunctata
Length 4mm. Small, rounded beetle. Wing cases hard, glossy, red with black spots on each side of mid-line. Eats huge numbers of greenfly so is useful in garden. Many species of ladybirds, with various numbers of spots; black and red or black and yellow.

Earwig
Forficula auricularia
Length 15mm. Insect with narrow, flattened body and small wing cases. Pincers at end of body, very curved in male, straighter in female. Very common, often in flowers and dark places. Harmless.

Wasp
Vespula vulgaris
Length 12mm. Nipped-in waist. Rear part of body with black and yellow markings, pointed and with a sting. Head has two, long *antennae*. Two pairs of wings, back pair much smaller than front. Very fond of sweet things and attracted to sweet foods or rotten fruit in summer.

Woodlouse
Oniscus asellus
Length 16mm. Flattened body, oval shape. Tough, jointed shell. Grey with lighter patches. Very common, but keeps to shady, slightly damp places such as garden rubbish or rotting wood.

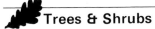

Trees & Shrubs

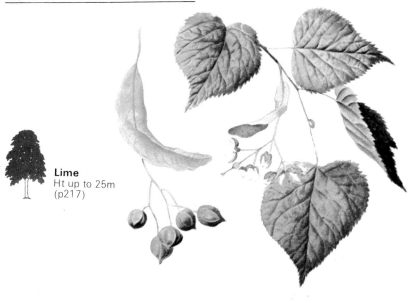

Lime
Ht up to 25m
(p217)

Plane
Ht up to 35m
(p217)

Maidenhair
Ht up to 30m
(p217)

Horse chestnut
Ht up to 25m
(p217)

Locust
Ht up to 27m
(p217)

Laburnum
Ht up to 7m
(p217)

Wych elm
Ht up to 40m
(p51)

Sycamore
Ht up to 30m
(p12)

Holly
Ht 5–8m
(p217)

Cedar
Ht up to 30m
(p218)

Tree of Heaven
Ht up to 28m
(p218)

Ornamental cherry
Ht up to 7m
(p218)

Ornamental almond
Ht 6 – 8m
(p218)

Date palm
Ht over 4·5m
(p218)

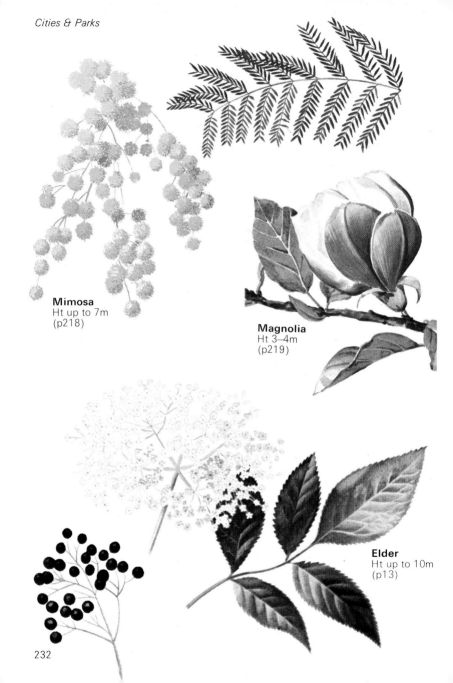

Mimosa
Ht up to 7m
(p218)

Magnolia
Ht 3–4m
(p219)

Elder
Ht up to 10m
(p13)

Rhododendron
Ht up to 18m
(p219)

Azalea
Ht up to 2m
(p219)

Bougainvillea
Ht up to 6m
(p219)

Buddleia
Ht 1 – 5m
(p219)

Rose
Ht up to 1·5m
(p220)

Box
Ht up to 6m
(p219)

Camellia
Ht up to 2·5m
(p219)

Herbs

Hedge bindweed
Ht up to 3m
(p220)

Oxford ragwort
Ht 200 – 300mm
(p220)

Field bindweed
L up to 750mm
(p220)

Tea-plant
Ht up to 2·5m
(p220)

Common mallow
Ht 450 – 900mm
(p220)

Wall rocket
Ht 150 – 600mm
(p220)

White dead-nettle
Ht 200 – 600mm
(p221)

Spear thistle
Ht 300mm – 1·5m
(p221)

Cocksfoot
Ht up to 1m
(p52)

Wall barley
Ht 60 – 600mm
(p221)

Meadow-grass
Ht 100 – 800mm
(p51)

Rye-grass
Ht 250 – 800mm
(p51)

Stinging nettle
Ht 300mm–1·5m
(p221)

Toadflax
Ht 300 – 800mm
(p221)

**Rosebay
willow-herb**
Ht 300mm – 1·2m
(p221)

Tulip
Ht up to 600mm
(p222)

Daffodil
Ht about 600mm
(p222)

Crocus
Ht 100mm
(p222)

Birds

Kestrel
L 338mm
(p222)

Pigeon
L 325mm
(p222)

Collared dove
L 315mm
(p222)

Jackdaw
L 330mm
(p54)

Robin
L 140mm
(p222)

Bluetit
L 112mm
(p223)

Wren
L 100mm
(p223)

Magpie
L 450mm
(p223)

House sparrow
L 145mm
(p223)

Blackbird
L 250mm
(p223)

Starling
L 215mm
(p223)

Pied wagtail
L 175mm
(p223)

Wood pigeon
L 400mm
(p223)

Black redstart
L 140mm
(p224)

Black-headed gull
L 375mm
(p224)

Song thrush
L 230mm
(p54)

Moorhen
L 320mm
(p88)

Cormorant
L 950mm
(p121)

Coot
L 370mm
(p88)

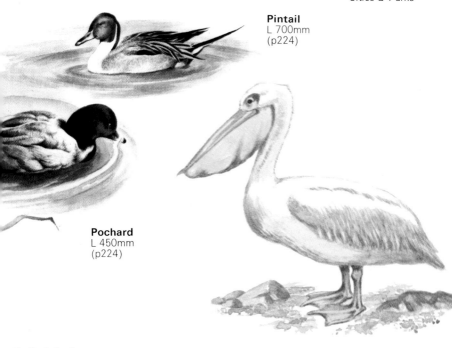

Pintail
L 700mm
(p224)

Pochard
L 450mm
(p224)

Tufted duck
L 425mm
(p224)

Pelican
L over 1·5m
(p224)

Mandarin duck
L 450mm
(p224)

245

Mammals

Hedgehog
BL 225 – 275mm
(p56)

Red squirrel
BL 195–280mm
(p19)

Grey squirrel
BL 245 – 300mm
(p19)

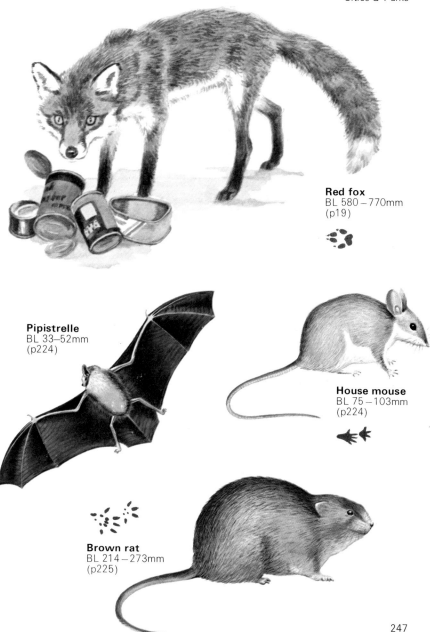

Red fox
BL 580–770mm
(p19)

Pipistrelle
BL 33–52mm
(p224)

House mouse
BL 75–103mm
(p224)

Brown rat
BL 214–273mm
(p225)

Fox terrier
Ht 300mm
(p225)

Spaniel
Ht up to 500mm
(p225)

Labrador retriever
Ht over 550mm
(p225)

Dachshund
Ht up to 250mm
(p225)

Poodle
Ht over 270mm
(p225)

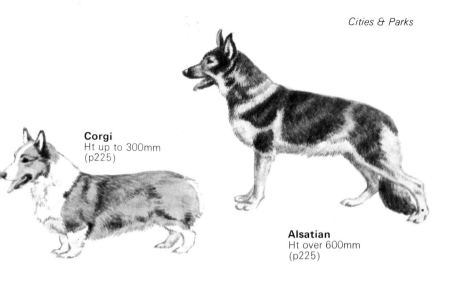

Corgi
Ht up to 300mm
(p225)

Alsatian
Ht over 600mm
(p225)

 **Invertebrates**

Two-spot ladybird
L 4mm
(p225)

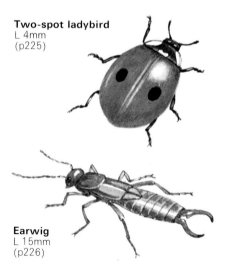

Wasp
L 12mm
(p226)

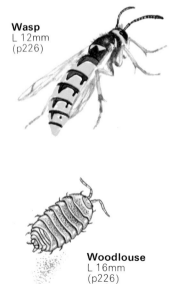

Earwig
L 15mm
(p226)

Woodlouse
L 16mm
(p226)

Index

Page numbers in **bold** type refer to illustrations.